The
BOLSHOI
BALLET
Story

•

FROM BALLET SCHOOL TO BOLSHOI THEATRE AND BACK
Y. BOCHARNIKOVA — M. GABOVICH

THE MAKING OF A BALLERINA
GALINA ULANOVA

INSIDE THE BOLSHOI BALLET
YURI SLONIMSKY

•

HELLER & HELLER

CONTENTS

THE METHOD

From Ballet School to Bolshoi Ballet and Back

By Y. Bocharnikova and M. Gabovich

THE MAKING OF A BALLERINA

By Galina Ulanova

INSIDE THE RUSSIAN BALLET

By Yuri Slonimsky

ILLUSTRATIONS

7

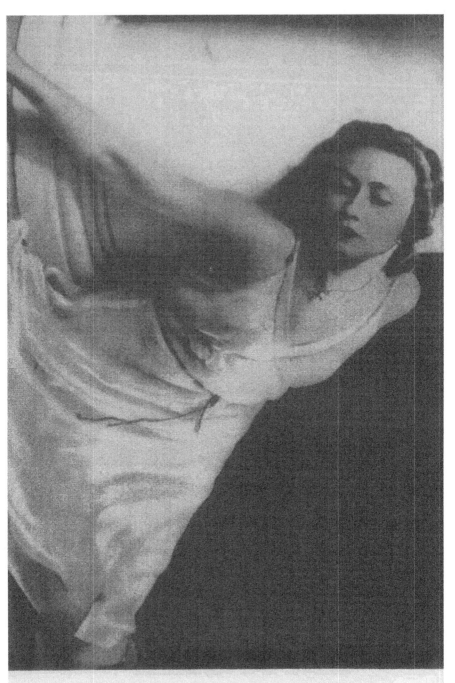

Foreword

The triumphal national tour of the Bolshoi Ballet Company has aroused renewed interest in Russian dance and dancers. Its impact on the American dance theatre says Lincoln Kirstein, General Director of the New York City Ballet—may be as great as that of the Diaghilev Ballets in 1916, which more or less brought about the founding of American ballet. Who and what are these Russian dancers? How are they trained? From what do they derive their incredible technical perfection? How, as dancers, have they succeeded in assimilating the Stanislavsky "Method"? And has this process produced a new type of ballet theater, as in *Romeo and Juliet?* Was it this provocative aspect of Soviet ballet that so struck our critics in their superlative enthusiasm?

The three important works on Soviet ballet included in this volume go a long way towards answering these questions.

The first work is a comprehensive study of the Bolshoi ballet school, describing every phase of the

school's life from admission requirements to Stanislav-
skian ballet techniques. Its co-authors are the school's
principal, Yelena Bocharnikova and its art director,
Mikhail Gabovich, leading dancer of the Bolshoi Ballet
for many years and creator of the role of Romeo in
Prokofief's *Romeo and Juliet*.

Galina Ulanova needs no introduction to anyone interested in ballet. She has been called "The wonder of
the world," by Harrison Salisbury of the New York
Times. Sublime at the age of fifty, she is a legend in
her own time. *The Making of a Ballerina* is her short
autobiography—as individual, as unmistakable as one of
her performances.

Yuri Slonimsky's *The Bolshoi Ballet* traces the per-
vasive growth of the company from its origins in a
Moscow Orphanage in 1773. He exposes the rich esthetic
underlying its vast repertoire and analyses it in detail.

These volumes are presented here condensed and
adapted for American readers.

Z. H.

Y. Bocharnikova
M. Gabovich

THE METHOD

From Ballet School to Bolshoi
Theatre and Back

Authors Note

IT IS NOT OUR AIM to tell the reader about all aspects of the work of the Moscow Ballet School. We shall not go into detail about each special subject, nor do we want this booklet to resemble a manual on classical ballet training. The specialist will look in vain for answers to the technical and aesthetic problems that may arise in his mind, for these deserve separate treatment elsewhere.

We want to give the reading public some appreciation of the work of the Bolshoi Theatre Ballet School, and if we succeed in giving a general picture of its work, we shall consider that our efforts have not been wasted.

So Near And Yet So Far

TWO OR THREE MINUTES' walk takes you from the Bolshoi Theatre to its school, one of the oldest in the Soviet Union, where future ballet dancers are trained. Geographically, its class-rooms are only a short distance from the theatre's stage, but what a long and arduous road of unremitting work and endless endeavour its pupils must travel before they join the Bolshoi Theatre company!

We enter a courtyard characteristic of old Moscow and see a four-storey house in no way remarkable externally. The sign at the entrance reads:

Moscow Ballet School of the Bolshoi Theatre
MINISTRY OF CULTURE OF THE U.S.S.R.

On the day of the entrance examinations the school's hall and corridors are full of children, with mothers and fathers helping them to take off their coats, adjust their dresses, tie their hair-ribbons and giving the last words of advice.

In their mind's eye the parents already see their small daughters or sons graduating from the school and be-

14

coming famous dancers. But the children themselves seem to care little about their future prospects: they just think it fun to dance and are eager to learn the beautiful art. Their hearts beat excitedly as they await their turn.

The entrance examinations are simple but extremely rigorous. It requires the highest discernment on the teachers' part to see potential dancers in little boys and girls, to detect their latent talent. All of those nine- and ten-year-old children are pretty and graceful. Their arms are supple, their legs slender, their backs straight, they move freely and rhythmically. But five or six years may bring a deterioration of the figure, raised shoulders, angular movements—in a word, realization that the girl or boy is unsuitable for ballet. On the other hand, a girl who seems to the examiners plain and not well-proportioned, may in the course of time develop into a first-rate dancer.

Only great experience can prevent mistakes in making the initial choice.

Whatever his or her appearance and abilities, a pupil must be strong and perfectly fit. A ballet dancer performs very hard physical work and no one who is weak can be a professional dancer. A dancer's pulse after a difficult variation is sometimes beating at the rate of 350 a minute. So all children are examined by doctors before being admitted to the entrance examinations. They carefully assess the child's physical condition, his eyesight, hearing, and nervous system; upon their verdict depends whether or not the child can be examined for professional qualifications.

During the examination a girl is requested to place her feet in ballet positions. The examiners inspect the arch of her instep, test her turn-out, her extension, suppleness, elevation, the plasticity of arm movement, her sense of rhythm. The observant eye of the specialist takes in everything about her. The teacher carefully raises the girl's leg in an *arabesque* in order to test her extension. She asks if the leg hurts. "No" is the shy reply.

"Then lift the leg a little higher," the teacher says. "Does it hurt now?" Once again "No"—but this time without conviction. The teachers know perfectly well that they will never hear a "Yes," but the tone is enough to show them when to stop.

At last the examinations are over. Thirty out of several hundred applicants are enrolled in the first year.

The school's aim is to train artists capable of revealing the rich inner world of man through artistic means, and not mere virtuoso dancers. Consequently, during their nine-year course the pupils, in addition to studying a great number of special subjects, take the usual secondary-school course and study various art subjects.

Moreover, all pupils take part in current performances at the Bolshoi Theatre and in concerts and performances arranged by the school from their very first year.

The children are thus introduced into the enchanted world of music and dancing. Step by step, their minds absorb the fundamentals of the artistic education so essential for ballet dancers.

At Lessons

THE OFFICE OF THE DIRECTOR of studies and the staff room are on the first floor; here too, is the time-table, displayed on a stand under glass. The school's varied work from day to day is here set down in black and white. We see that classes are held from 9 a.m. to 6 p.m. A feature that strikes anyone studying the time-table for the first time is that Classical Dance occurs here daily and takes up two academic hours in every class, altogether 90 minutes. No other subject receives so much attention as this basic discipline. Another regular feature of the daily time-table is of course Dinner. But a visit to the dining-hall shows that the pupils are not so unanimous in their devotion to this function as to the classical dance. While junior pupils are seen attacking their three-course dinner with complete unconcern and seem to enjoy particularly the dessert, older pupils, especially girls, approach it with caution. They curb their youthful appetites and stick to the diet; like grown ballerinas, they want to preserve their slim figures.

We go back to the time-table to choose the classes we would like to visit. There is a wide choice in the three main groups of subjects—Special, General and Art. Such subjects as arithmetic, biology, Russian, geography, drawing, history, physics, foreign languages, the history

of the West-European theatre, the theory and history
of music, and many others, do not particularly interest
us at present. We prefer Classical Dance.

On entering the hall where the first-year pupils are
receiving instruction we plunge into an atmosphere of
great concentration. Fifteen little girls in light dresses
are standing at the bar intent on their exercise. If asked,
the teacher will tell you that all of them arrive "at
unearthly hours," long before 9 a.m. when the lesson begins. But first-year pupils have done that for generations.
We watch future ballerinas being initiated into the
rudiments of classical ballet. The first thing to master
are the Five Positions—the positions of the feet most
convenient for starting different *pas* from. But they are far
from easy: in the First Position, for instance, the feet
must be turned out completely, touching each other only
with the backs of the heels and forming a continuous
straight line; in the Fifth, the turned-out feet are placed
parallel, the toe of one foot touching the heels of the
other. The teacher demonstrates the steps, patiently
checking the girls' "placing" and correcting those who
do not get everything right the first time.

The next exercise is the *plié* performed in all the Five
Positions. The teacher watches her pupils attentively,
keeping an observant eye not only on their legs: now
and again you hear, "Your back, Natasha!" or "Don't
let your arms hang limp, Katya!" Some of the girls are
more gifted than the others, but all these Natashas and
Katyas are extremely serious and concentrated during
the lessons, which they all see as the road towards their

18

supreme aim in life.

Next door second-year boys and girls are receiving instruction in historical dances. They go over the basic steps of the polka and waltz in couples. The teachers had a lot of trouble to get the boys to offer their arms to their partners. At that age boys' contempt for girls is so deep-rooted that a teacher has to resort to various "diplomatic moves" to make a twelve-year-old cavalier show "knightly gallantry" towards the "lady" with whom he performs a period ballroom dance.

But at the sound of the interval bell they immediately lose their "courtly manners" and rush along the corridors and down the stairs into the courtyard for ten minutes of play. Some, however, are of a more serious turn and prefer the Pioneer Room, the place for quiet, more thoughtful games and activities. Ten minutes is enough for a spell at some indoor game—even for a lightning game of chess. Then there are flowers for the girls to water and goldfish to feed. In the evening the editors of the school's wall newspaper meet to prepare the next issue—to write a critical or an approving article, to draw cartoons of those who "break the rules."

In the school itself, just as in any other educational establishment, the problem of discipline requires constant attention from the entire teaching staff, but it all but vanishes as soon as the pupils come to the Bolshoi Theatre to take part in an opera or ballet. The most mischievous child changes beyond all recognition as soon as he finds himself in the atmosphere of concentrated creative work and becomes infected with the sense of collective responsibility for the performance. Participation from an early age in the work of a large theatrical team exercises a highly beneficial influence on the pupils' behaviour and upbringing.

But the break is over and we resume our inspection of the school. We hear the strains of Asafiev's *Fountain of Bakhchisarai* coming from a hall. A group of Albanian youths and girls are rehearsing Act III of that ballet by choreographer R. Zakharov. They are preparing for their graduation concert which will show what they have learned during their five years at the Ballet.

These three young men and three young women came to Moscow when they were 15 or 16 years old. Although they had never seen a classical ballet, dancing was a passion with them and each was a talented performer of their native folk dances in amateur dance groups.

Their training at the Moscow Ballet School started from scratch. For five years they worked hard, studying classical and folk dancing, acting, the history of ballet and other art subjects, the Russian language and literature, and so on. They had an equally keen interest in the methods of teaching dancing and in choreography.

Albania's first professional ballet dancers graduated last year. Without a doubt these first seeds will produce many new shoots and Albania will have a classical ballet of her own: the land of the mountain eagle will in a few years see Chaikovsky's white swan.

Entering the class-room of the seventh-year pupils, we find them studying Russian literature. Our ears drink in the music of Pushkin's lyric verse:

At Lessons

The Khan returned to the Crimea
And to commemorate Maria
He bade a marble font be reared
In a lone corner of the yard.
The water from the fountain gushed
And tear-like drops fell to the ground.
Its mournful sound was never hushed. . . .

It would be safe to assume that most of them first learned the plot of Pushkin's *Fountain of Bakhchisaraı* not from the poem itself but from the ballet, a truly artistic choreographic interpretation of the spirit and lyricism of the poem. As they listen they see in their mind's eye the "sorrowful Maria"—Ulanova—and once more their hearts fill with pity for her tragic fate. Their literary studies give new meaning to the image they know from the stage.

You are again reminded of the bond between litera-ture and ballet in the mime class. Here final-year pupils are studying how to render the emotions of Romeo and Juliet at their first meeting. What is the logic (and, consequently, the truth) of their stage behaviour? How are the actors to show the birth of their love and convey the great significance this meeting has for the subse-quent fate of the young lovers?

These are the problems confronting the pupils as they study the Ball scene. The class watches with rapt attention as Juliet is struck motionless at the sight of Romeo. You *believe* in the sincerity of her rapture and happiness—a happiness tinged with foreboding of the tragic fate in store for the two "star-crossed lovers."

Classical Dance Comes First

THE CLASSICAL DANCE is the foundation of all studies in the Ballet School.

It takes the pupils nine long years to study, one after another, all the elements of classical ballet, until they become perfect masters of the technique of the dance. At the same time they work on the expressive aspect of dancing, so that technique becomes art, creating the choreographic image. Clearly, no image can be created without perfect mastery of the classical system.

But what *is* this system? How did it take shape? How can it impart poetic and artistic expressiveness to the human body? The ability to dance and to express emotions through the medium of movement is inherent in the human body. But in order that the dance might become an art, there had to be evolved a system co-ordinating motions and gestures just as harmony co-ordinates sounds in music. This system had to be the objective language of the art.

In the evolution of the art of dancing the system acquired certain laws born of artistic practice and of the union between aesthetic requirements and the physical potentialities of the human body.

Classical ballet has unified movements of a very varied character and created a universal plastic language which an artist uses to build up a choreographic image.

Classical Dance Comes First

The system of classical dance steps and gestures is made up of carefully selected movements of the human body, abstracted from their every-day application, as well as of folk-dance elements and mime gestures. The *arabesque*, for example, is a derivative of chance movements which occur a countless number of times in every-day life, the most convincing of which were selected, generalized and given the form of the acknowledged classical dance pose.

The romantic approach to life characteristic of the thirties of the last century gave rise to the aesthetic idea of flight associated with an airy being leaving earth and striving upwards, which found its realization in dancing *sur les pointes*. The introduction of the *pointes* in turn made possible new technical achievements and brought about a highly developed *terre-à-terre* technique, such as the *fouettées chainés, tours de force,* etc.

The strength of classical ballet as an art lies in its ability to give expression to human thoughts and emotions in a way at once poetically generalized and concrete.

As Rodin put it, the art of the sculptor lies in the ability to divest a piece of marble of all that is superfluous. Ulanova likewise divests her characters of all that is superfluous and accidental. Her dancing is full of meaning and beauty.

Man is the subject of art, and the dancer devotes her exquisitely lyrical talent, her fine and sincere acting, her impeccable technique, plasticity and timing to the one aim of showing the wealth of human emotions, passions and aspirations. Galina Ulanova's art is the highest expression of these qualities, which are characteristic of the Russian school of classical dancing.

The beauty and poetry of ballet are achieved by means of an "alphabet"—a definite system of classical dance movements. The subject Classical Dance as taught at the Ballet School consists in studying this "alphabet," using its letters to make words, and the words to make stanzas of whole poems—ballets.

The programme for the first year includes placing of the body, legs, head and development of a correct *port de bras,* as well as exercises at the bar and centre practice. Work on developing conscious expressiveness goes side by side with technical training from the very outset.

As a result of constant training, the muscles develop and the pupils learn to co-ordinate their movements into a harmonious whole.

The technical aspect of the young dancers' training becomes more complex from year to year. They master various turns, more complex steps of elevation and *batterie,* while familiar exercises are performed at a more rapid tempo and dance sequences are introduced.

Technique is further perfected in the senior classes. Here special attention is paid to the development of the artistic individuality of each pupil. Technical difficulties are more numerous and the *enchainements* become more complicated. Fragments from ballets are studied.

In the final year the whole programme is gone over once more in a technically integrated form and at a quick tempo, emphasis being laid on combining expressive acting and technical virtuosity. The pupils study solo and ballerina variations and whole acts from bal lets.

The classical dance lessons take place in well-lit spacious halls with a mirror wall. Strict discipline, concentration and hard work are demanded from the outset. Even the first two or three months of training give uniformity, precision, perfection of rhythm and a particular *dance quality* to the movements.

During the first lessons the exercises are performed at the bar, but later the lesson is divided into two parts —bar exercises and centre practice.

In the senior and final-year classes purely technical tasks are combined with artistic ones. The students perform varied and complex dance *enchainements,* repeating them many times to achieve expressiveness, precision and fluency. Under the guidance of the teacher they correct their mistakes. They always bear in mind that they must not merely listen to the music but also interpret its emotional message through their movements.

Besides indicating the type of exercises in junior, medium and senior classes, besides setting down the sequence in which dance elements should be studied in each class, the methods of teaching the classical dance attach great importance to training the pupils in a spirit of strict and conscious discipline, instilling in them the need for constant and persistent physical effort and attaining finish and perfection in every movement. The pupils know that the exercises they study in class will be transformed on the stage into the language of choreography, and that carelessness in mastering the elements of the classical dance, perfunctory movements and mistakes, no matter how big or small, will invariably be repeated on the stage, not merely ruining the dance but distorting the choreographic image and marring the ballet as a whole.

The habit of regular and continuous practice is formed and kept alive by the lessons in classical dance throughout the nine years of study. Thus, the whole body, the entire mechanism of motion is kept in a state of professional readiness, in what is known as "the perfect dance form."

The classical dance lessons also play an important part in the aesthetic education of the pupils. In some pupils the teachers may find affectation in executing the dance movement, mannerisms and posing, attempts to "show off" or other manifestations of bad taste. All attempts of this kind are ruthlessly eradicated.

But while they train their pupils in the spirit of severe classicism, the teachers do not consider the system of the classical dance as a rigid set of rules allowing of no alternation and exhausting all the potentialities of the human body. They are always on the alert for anything new that appears in the theatre with its new themes and heroes; they readily borrow folk-dance elements which can enrich the classical ballet.

The classical dance lessons are also a means of musical education: the music to which the exercises and dances are performed is selected in order to develop the pupils' sense of rhythm, creative imagination and musical taste.

Moreover, since the study of the classical dance is intimately linked with music, and since the music the pupils hear at the lessons has profound meaning and is highly emotional, it stimulates choreographic thought and imagination.

Piano lessons contribute a still greater share to the musical education of the future dancers. The programme is drawn up in such a way as to acquaint the pupils with the works of Russian and West European classics, as well as of Soviet and modern foreign composers. Folk music is also studied here. Dances, familiarizing the pupils with different measures and rhythms, naturally have a prominent place in the selection of pieces which the pupils have to play.

As their artistic horizons broaden, the pupils learn to penetrate deeper into the meaning of the works performed, to make their own interpretations truthful, meaningful, expressive and technically perfect.

Along with training in the fundamentals of the classical dance, senior pupils study the art of partnering. First they master the technique of hold and lift, then they perform études in the form of classical *pas de deux,* which at a later stage are superseded by excerpts from classical ballets. All this enables the pupils to achieve harmony between the technical and expressive aspects of the classical dance.

With unflagging persistence the teacher demands from the young artists perfect plastic form, complete unity between their movements and the musical phrase, and psychological justification of the whole scene.

27

Dances of Many Nations

Upon entering the dance studio where the lesson in Folk and Character Dance is in progress you find yourself in an entirely different world. *Battements,* beats, *pirouettes* and tours are performed here in a new manner that gives them a national flavour. A scintillating technique of the squatting *prisyadka,* heel-work and leaps is added to the ballet vocabulary.

The Character Dance course at the Ballet School has several aims. First, the pupils must master the character dances known as academic—Spanish, Italian, Hungarian, Polish, and others—which are lavishly introduced into most classical ballets and operas. These dances were created by such great masters as Petipa, Gorsky and Fokine, and it is therefore clear why Soviet choreographers carefully preserve this classical legacy. But at the same time the school's teachers in an effort to restore their original genuine folk character strive to remove the layer of clichés and even bad taste which has accumulated over the course of the years on some of the academic dances of the classic repertoire.

But since the Ballet School trains artists who are to perform not only in the old classic repertoire but also in new ballets, some of them based on modern themes, it is perfectly natural that the character-dance syllabus

28

should include a study of the contemporary folk dances of the peoples of the Soviet Union. So the pupils of the school study Russian, Ukrainian, Byelorussian, Georgian, Uzbek, Armenian, Moldavian and Tajik dances, as well as those of many others peoples.

While learning the dances of the various peoples, the pupils learn about the life and history of each people, as well as the origin of the steps and movements in their dances.

The study of character dancing includes both exercises at the bar and centre practice. The former are meant to train and develop the muscles, joints and tendons of the legs and arms while the latter, as we have said, are usually in the form of études, in the performance of which the pupils master style, develop expressive acting and learn to create truly national characters through the medium of the dance. The experience of Soviet ballet has shown that this system of teaching folk and character dances yields exceptionally good results.

The experience accumulated by the Ballet School in teaching folk dances has made it a centre where the traditions of its stage interpretation are preserved and developed, a repository of the achievements of choreographers in this field. Choreographers of new ballets come here in search of material.

The teaching of folk and character dances influences the ballet in another way: besides employing dances containing the vivid and vital elements of original but artistically adapted folk dances as divertissements in

new ballets Soviet choreographers introduce these elements into the classical dance, thus enriching it with
new and graphic expressive means.

For all the wealth and universality of the classical
dance vocabulary we today cannot help feeling that
purely classical compositions lack features indicating the
time of the action and national characteristics. Soviet
choreographers therefore preserve the specific founda-
tions of the classical dance, with all its wealth of expressive means, and at the same time, use the elements
of folk dances to make the choreographic image more
concrete, true-to-life and convincing.

The Study of the Past

THERE ARE MANY BALLETS in the repertoire which represent the life and customs of the past; they often contain interesting ball-room dances—the solemn and ceremonious Dance with the Cushion in *Romeo and Juliet* based on the steps of the branle, a very old dance, or the Saraband, a stately court dance, in *Flame of Paris,* danced by ladies in farthingales and cavaliers in powdered wigs.

The future dancers must know and be able to perform the dances of the most varied periods, nations and styles. In the Historical Dance course they study court and ball-room dances from the 16th to the 19th century, as well as the stage behaviour characteristic of the period. The pupils learn to "commune with their partners," in Stanislavsky's words, in the manner accepted at a given period, to wear historical costumes, hats, to use the sword, etc.

Historical dance is studied for four years—from the first to the third year, and then after an interval of five years in the final year.

First-year pupils are taught the rudiments of historical dances, their simplest elements. The teachers' aim at this stage is to develop in the girls and boys the "feel" of the dance, grace, elasticity and co-ordination. The children dance both *legato* and *staccato,* they learn the turns in the polka and the waltz. Then come bows, curtseys, the *pas glissés, pas chaussés, pas élevés,* the galop, etc. Lastly, they study the basic steps of the polonaise, the polka, and other dances. The teachers pay special attention to the holding of the body, the legs, the head, the shoulders, and a proper *port de bras.*

During the second year the performance of previously learned dances is perfected, the dances themselves are given in a more complicated form and a number of new ones learned. The steps of the polonaise become more complex, and both the polka and the waltz are learned in their combined forms. The new dances include the various figures of the quadrille, the mazurka, the mignon, the Hungarian dance, etc.

The third year brings the polishing of what has already been learned, while further work is done on technique and expression, as well as on new dances. These include the 18th century gavotte, the figure mazurka, the Cracovienne, the *pas d'Espagne,* the *pas de quatre,* the Moldavaneska and the old Russian slow dance.

In the final year of study the styles of dancing in the 16th-19th centuries are studied, together with the artistic and expressive approach to their stage presentation. The pupils perform études in period behaviour. The most difficult parts of the syllabus are 16th-century dances, such as the branle and the pavane. While not remarkable from the point of view of technique, the dances call for an impeccable style and manner of execution. In the study of these dances the études in proper stage manners both during the dance itself and before and after it (the entrance, the exit, the salutation, the invitation to the dance) are of very great importance.

During their last year the pupils learn the best examples of historical dances from ballets created by classical masters and by Soviet choreographers.

Visits to museums, where the pupils study paintings, sculptures and drawings, and objects of every-day use from the past are an important aid to their study of historical dances.

Dance Language And The Stanislavsky Method

THE APPEARANCE of new themes and new heroes in ballet and the problem of teaching young dancers the art of acting have suggested the necessity of applying Stanislavsky's method to choreography.

This method, used by many dramatic actors, is a scientific analysis of the laws governing the actor's creative process. According to Stanislavsky, to work on a character means to give an artistic interpretation of the "inner life of a human spirit" through the medium of the behaviour and actions of an actor on the stage. The verisimilitude of the dramatic action, Stanislavsky says, depends in the first place on the correct comprehension of the main idea of a work. He calls this the super-objective on which the attention of all the actors must be focussed. On the basis of this, each individual actor must find the super-objective of his part and by consistent action contribute to the achievement of the super-objective of the whole play.

Stanislavsky holds that belief in the truth of the given circumstances (the circumstances of the character's dramatic life) is one of the most important laws of creation. Once he believes in his character, the actor decides how he would act if he found himself in the supposed circumstances.

In order to acquire this belief, an actor must be able to concentrate, i.e., forget his real self and, without dividing his attention, enter the mental and emotional world of the character he portrays; an actor must possess developed powers of observation; he must master the technique of shaking off forces interfering with the free expression of his creative self. In a word, Stanislavsky calls for an acting technique which enables an actor to behave on the stage as simply and unaffectedly as in ordinary life.

The application of the Stanislavky method to choreography has long been the subject of discussions in ballet circles. The way this can be done is not yet clear.

The special nature of the art, based as it is on music, must of necessity amend Stanislavsky's methods of training "dancing actors." Stanislavsky himself, who devoted much time to opera, was perfectly aware of these peculiarities of ballet.

The emotional make-up of every ballet role is predetermined by the music. Stanislavsky pointed out that music was the language of feelings. He required opera and ballet actors to translate the language of passions into that of actions. He urged them to "borrow" their actions from the music so that while the actor was engaged in performing these actions he should experience the feelings inherent in the music. Another characteristic of ballet is that the actor-dancer cannot create the "score" of his movements (actions) at will: not only is his behaviour in time determined by the music; he also has a ready-made choreographic "text"—the pattern of his actions in space.

These characteristics of the art of ballet dictate the chief requirements which a dancer must meet—to be able to understand, analyze and feel the music and translate its emotional message into the language of the dance.

The center of attention at the dramatic art lessons are mime and dance études which develop the pupils' ability to base their actions expressed in movement—on the emotions and meaning of the music. These are both suggested by the tutor and improvised by the pupils themselves.

During the first year of drama training (in one of the senior classes) the pupils study the fundamentals of the Stanislavsky method, developing stage attention, imagination, communion and interaction with partners, etc. They perform training exercises for all of these elements in "given circumstances."

Further work in the mime class consists in studying concrete ballet roles in excerpts, scenes or *pas de deux*. But first the ballet as a whole is analyzed in detail, its idea and super-objective are defined and the main conflict determining the whole action clearly stated. The music, the dramaturgy and the choreography of the ballet are also carefully analyzed.

When an excerpt or a scene from a ballet is taken up, its bearing on the whole as well as the significance in the development of the characters is discussed.

Dance Language—The Stanislavsky Method

In the last year of drama training the pupils work on the creation of an integrated character in a ballet production. An important feature of the lessons at this stage is the perfection of the choreographic form and the plastic pattern of the part.

However, we must say once more that the problem of the application of Stanislavsky's system to the art of ballet is not quite clear and that the efficacy of this method of training young actors is being tested in practice. Only practice can suggest changes in the methods of studying the technique of acting for the different genres of ballet (lyrical, heroic, comedy, etc.). So far, only one thing is clear: the extensive and varied experience in drama technique accumulated on the Russian legitimate stage and summed up in the Stanislavsky method is a treasure-house from which young dancer-actors can gain much that is useful in the creation of choreographic characters.

A character in choreography has many specific features and differs in many respects from a character in the drama theatre. It is a task of choreographers to preserve and assert the specific musical and plastic expressiveness of the human body which is the foundation of the art of dancing.

Stage Appearances

However diligent the pupils may be in polishing their exercises, they could not become full-fledged professionals without practice, without exercising their creative faculties on the stage. That is why appearances on the stage are so important in training young artists.

The school's experience clearly demonstrates that stage appearances help to reveal the personality of each pupil, to develop his plastic and histrionic expressiveness and his mastery of stage presence.

The programmes of all special subjects throughout the course provide for the study of parts in which the pupils must appear on the stage. The pupils study the current repertoire (both solo and ensemble dances), and whole scenes and acts from such ballets as *Swan Lake, Giselle, La Bayadere, Esmeralda, The Corsair, Don Quixote, La Fille Mal Gardée, Coppélia,* etc.

The dance items learned in different special classes are performed at school concerts which are a method of checking progress in special subjects. The best items are then included in the programme of the annual public concerts.

Dance numbers, both academic and concert, are arranged by the teachers of special subjects, by choreographers of the Bolshoi and other theaters, and also by choreographers from folk dance ensembles: Vasily Vainonen, Leonid Lavrovsky, Kasyan Goleizovsky, Igor Moiseyev, Leonid Yakobson, Mansur Kalmaletdinov, and others.

When we say that the Ballet School and the Bolshoi Theatre are one family, it is not mere figure of speech: the school's performances are given on the stage of the Bolshoi Filial and the pupils participate as a matter of course in the opera and ballet performances of the theatre.

Clearly, since the pupils prepare very seriously for the public concerts, polishing each dance item and trying to achieve a professional standard of execution, a ballet performance by them included in the theatre's repertoire must be a true work of art, the work of professional artists.

Three of the school's ballet productions—*Nutcracker*, *La Fille Mal Gardée* and *The Baby Stork*—have been permanent features of the Bolshoi repertoire.

Nutcracker, one of the three ballet masterpieces of Chaikovsky, has been running at the Bolshoi Filial for more than five years. It is given several times a season with new casts. Its story and characters are such that pupils of all classes—from first years to final years—can take part.

Several years ago the school produced Hertel's *La Fille Mal Gardée*, a very popular classical ballet, which was for a long time a permanent feature of the repertoire.

The third ballet staged and performed by the school was *The Baby Stork* to the music of Klebanov, with choreography by three young Bolshoi dancers, former pupils of the school, Alexander Radunsky, Nikolai Popko and Lev Pospekhin. The ballet, their debut as choreographers, was on a contemporary theme.

The Baby Stork was intended to solve important educational and other problems, such as friendship among children of different nations, collective work, kindness to animals, all understandable to children and vividly and truthfully mirrored in the ballet.

An instructive and gay work full of warm, sincere feeling and mellow humour, *The Baby Stork* was invariably successful with children's audiences.

Participation in "real" performances, whether at the school or the Bolshoi Theatre, increases the pupils' sense of responsibility and encourages them to strive after perfection in technique and acting. It is, in fact, an excellent school in itself.

Seventy-six pupils from the second up to the final-year class take part in Bolshoi Theatre performances of *Cinderella*, 59 in *The Sleeping Beauty*, 48 in *Red Poppy*, 20 in *Swan Lake* and *Don Quixote*, 14 in the opera *Sadko*, 12 in *Faust, Don Juan, Rigoletto*—altogether in 15 ballets and about a dozen operas.

Dancing and acting in opera and ballet performances aid the pupils' artistic development and at the same time educate them, although more slowly and imperceptibly. When they come into contact with famous dancers and watch their performances, they profit by their elder comrades' stage experience, technical skill, acting and artistic taste.

This combination of study and appearance on the stage is the main characteristic of the system used at the Ballet School.

Final Examinations

The day of the final examinations is an exciting and solemn event at the Ballet School.

In the morning small knots of young people are seen in the corridors; the class-rooms, usually ringing with voices, are silent. Those who are to show what they have learned during the nine years at school have come first. All are naturally agitated, because the examining commission consists of leading figures from the ballet world. Their teachers are equally excited.

The examinations take place in the school's largest hall. There is a long table covered with a green cloth at which the examiners sit. Here is Yury Fayer, chief ballet conductor of the Bolshoi Theatre; this stocky bespectacled, lively man has for 40 years conducted ballet performances at the Bolshoi and is one of the greatest connoisseurs of the art. Galina Ulanova enters with an air of thoughtfulness and concentration. She has a gift for correctly assessing the potentialities of future ballet stars. The vivacious Olga Lepeshinskaya, too, is a member of the commission.

The public is not admitted, but somehow the eight-year pupils who are to undergo the same experience in a year's time have found their way in.

The pianist takes her seat at the piano, the school's

principal gives the signal and the examination begins. The girls in simple flowing *tuniques* line up along the three walls of the hall (the youths' turn will come after them). The girls perform a long exercise at the bar, based on the elements of the classical dance. This alphabet of classic ballet enables the young performers to show their precision of execution and purity of line. In their approach to this part of the examination teachers and examiners are guided by Stanislavsky's precept— bring every elementary exercise to perfection, to the highest degree of artistry. Then center practice is performed by groups of four and five. The brief *adagio* is followed by a grand *adagio,* then come *allegro,* leaps and an exercise *sur les pointes.*

These latter exercises form a sequence of dance movements enabling the examiners to form an idea of the qualities possessed by the future dancers, of their line, their *aplomb,* the gracefulness of the girls and the strength and dexterity of the young men—in short the degree to which the young artists have mastered the classical technique.

Exercises are all very well, but the examiners cannot pass their final judgement on the artistry, musicality and technical virtuosity of the pupils based on exercises alone. The complete picture is obtained after the graduation concert and it sometimes happens that the concert produces startling revelations and makes the examiners revise their opinions.

At the examination a girl may seem to lack personality and fail to excite interest. But at the concert, if the teachers were careful to choose a dance capable of revealing her artistic personality, she makes an entirely different impression, so that the examiners are quite certain of their decision.

, So when the teachers decide on the dance excerpt to be performed by each pupil they bear in mind the wise saying, "Measure seven times before cutting once." Examinations are quickly followed by the public concert of the graduates, usually at the Bolshoi Filial. All the graduating pupils appear in the concert, enabling the examiners to pronounce the final judgement on their professional qualities.

The question of who will be accepted into the Bolshoi ballet company, too, is decided after the graduation concert. The Bolshoi Theatre takes only the very best, and, of course, there are disappointments and tears as many see their hopes of becoming Bolshoi artists shattered. But, fortunately, the Bolshoi Theatre is not the only one where a young ballet dancer can work and create.

All the opera houses of the country need dancers, and every graduate of the Ballet School is certain to be engaged. They are to be found in Leningrad, Tbilisi, Yerevan, Sverdlovsk, Novosibirsk, Kiev, Perm, Riga, Tashkent, and many other cities. Many of them become members of the State Folk Dance Ensemble headed by Igor Moiseyev, also a former pupil of the Ballet School, of the *Beryozka* Ensemble, or of other professional dance groups.

No matter in what capacity they work—as dancers,

ballet-masters or teachers—graduates of the Moscow Ballet School bring with them a consummate technique and make an important contribution to the progress of Soviet ballet.

From Ballet School To Bolshoi Theatre And Back

W<small>HAT IS THE SECRET</small> of the Ballet School's success in training highly-qualified professional dancers? The answer lies in the many-sided and constant links between the school and the Bolshoi Theatre. This in no way detracts from the importance of the educational work within the school itself. But it breathes the creative atmosphere of the Bolshoi Theatre and its educational work is largely determined by the theatre's influence. Volumes could be written about the interchange of the artistic tradition in Soviet ballet. But it would all be in vain without reference to the individuals who are the exponents of that tradition.

The school's staff is for the most part composed of past or present Bolshoi Theatre dancers.

Almost all of them were trained at the Moscow Ballet School. On graduating they were accepted in the Bolshoi ballet company and, after gaining experience on its stage, after years of creative work, return to train new generations of dancers. Teachers whose work is bearing abundant fruit include Nikolai Tarasov, Asaf Messerer, Galina Petrova, Sulamith Messerer, Vera Vasilyeva, Li-

dia Rafailova, Alexander Rudenko, Margarita Rozhdest-
venskaya-Vasilyeva, Tamara Tkachenko, Alexei Zhukov,
Vladimir Golubin, Yury Kondratov, Alexander Lapauri,
Mansur Kamaletdinov and Tatyana Ustinova. Among
those, too, are the most experienced teachers of the
classical dance, Yelizaveta Gerdt, Maria Kozshukhova
and Marina Semyonova, graduates of the Leningrad
Ballet School and former artists of the Leningrad ballet
and Moscow ballet. They enjoy deserved respect at the
Moscow school, to which they have brought the finest
traditions of the Leningrad school.

The different personalities of these artists naturally
leave their mark on the personalities of their pupils.
At the same time the teachers do their best to bring out
and develop the individual qualities of each pupil.

That is why young dancers from the Moscow Ballet
School differ in their personalities and in their manner
of dancing, although all belong to the same school of
Soviet choreography.

The history of the Moscow Ballet School almost two
centuries long exemplifies the creative ties between the
school and the Bolshoi Theatre. The pupils, artists and
teachers are constantly moving between two points—the
school and the theatre, and then again the school—and
this feature of the school's development has made an
important contribution to the development of the whole
Russian school of classical dancing.

*   *   *

Y. Bocharnikova — M. Gabowich

Yes, it is only a few minutes walk from the Ballet School to the Bolshoi Theatre.

The distance is short, but what a long and arduous road of unremitting work and ceaseless endeavour its pupils travel before they win the right to the title of artistes of the Bolshoi Theatre, of Soviet ballet dancers.

Galina Ulanova

THE MAKING
OF A BALLERINA

I DID NOT REALLY WISH to be a ballet dancer. True, my first visit to the theatre fired my imagination, but I was not swept off my feet by that strong impulse for a stage career which precipitated so many to the footlights.

The first performance I saw was, of course, a ballet. My father, régisseur of the ballet troupe at the Imperial Mariinsky Theatre in St. Petersburg, took me to see *The Sleeping Beauty.* All would have gone off well if at the appearance of the Lilac Fairy I had not cried out at the top of my voice: "That's mama, my mama!" The general embarrassment was great and the people sitting in the actors' box were quite shocked—why I could not understand. Had I not spoken the truth? The Lilac Fairy *was* my mother. She looked so enchanting in her lovely dress, her movements were so graceful, that I could not restrain my childish delight. I longed for everyone to know that the illustrious fairy was my own mother, mine and no one else's.

Such was the theatre's first impact on me, made through the being I knew and loved best. And so warm and lasting has been that impression that to this day I cannot think of *The Sleeping Beauty,* or even ballet in general, without calling to mind that early vision of the Lilac Fairy. To my own performances in *The Sleeping Beauty* and other ballets lay a long road of years at school and years of artistic adolescence. I set out on that road when the greatest social revolution in history took place.

And perhaps because I lacked prevision in the matter of my calling I "wept bitterly for fear when I was taken a stranger to my new home"*—the Petrograd School of Choreography. I was taken there out of sheer necessity, and not only for educational reasons. The years following the Revolution were strenuous years and my parents were always busy; in addition to the ballet performances at the theatre, they gave three recitals a night before film audiences. Free recitals at cinema houses had become a regular practice with the leading actors and dancers of the academic theatres in their endeavour to bring art nearer to the people. I remember how, frozen and sleepy, I was carried in my father's arms, from one of these recitals, through the bitter cold, snow-swept city. As there was nobody to look after me at home, my parents could do nothing but take me along with them.

There comes a picture to my mind of my mother changing into her ballet shoes from clumsy felt boots and tying the pink ribbons with stiff, numb fingers in a cold little cubby-hole behind the screen. I remember her adjusting her crisp, tarlatan *tutus* and coming out on the stage platform with a smile. But the smile did not deceive me; I saw clearly how fatigued mother was and what strain it cost her to dance. Is it surprising then that upon being told that I would be taught to dance I should reply most emphatically: "I don't want to!" Yet I found myself soon enough studying and board-

* Pushkin, *Eugene Onegin*

ing at the ballet school, because under the circumstances it was the easiest way out for my parents.

However, at the very first lesson, I pleaded with my mother, who was our teacher, to take me home. This I did over and over again, until mother promised to take me from the school at the New Year. I was delighted, and settled down to my lessons. But then shortly before the happy day I caught myself thinking that I was not so anxious to quit after all. I had made friends, among them Tanya Vecheslova and other girls. I was being taught by my own mother and many other good instructors. And though I had difficulty with the exercises at the *barre*, I felt that I had learned something. A childish pride in my achievements awakened in me an appreciation and respect for what we were doing at school.

I was growing fond of the lessons, of the rhythmic movements, and the system we followed in the exercises. Moreover, I was flattered to be singled out, along with Tanya Vecheslova and a few other girls, from among the whole lot of Class-One pupils to dance in a real ballet at the Academic Opera and Ballet Theatre. True, "dance" is hardly the word for the few "crawling movements" we performed as lady-birds in Drigo's *Caprices of a Butterfly*. All the same this *"début"* gave me my first joy at the thought that, thank goodness, I had made no slips, had followed the music and the count as I had been taught in class. Afterwards I got my first "role," that of a bird in Rimsky-Korsakov's *Snow Maiden*. We children had quite a clear idea of what the fairy-tale was about and what was happening on the stage. We

53

clustered eagerly around beautiful Spring and the clear tinkling of the music seemed to bring to us the freshness of the morning and the first breath of warmth.

We were children and it is with the psychology of children that we tackled the problems presented by our "roles." It was then quite easy for me to believe, or clearly imagine, that I was a lady-bird or a little spring bird. Children will let their imagination run away with them. What a pity that this childish credulity in the make-believe world of the stage, called for by Stanislavsky all his life, is so difficult to retain in later years, and that one must put in so much effort before one can really "live" a character, that is, believe in it so utterly, as to make the audience believe in it too. To a great measure, in my early "roles," I was merely a child at play, to whom the world of imagination was more real than life.

However, more than anything else, even in childhood, I regarded my performances as work with which I was charged and which I must do to the best of my ability. And to do my very best I *must* go through a daily grind. I must . . . the sense of obligation that went with these words had made me a hard plodder long before I had a real inclination to be a creative artist, long before I came to understand the problems inherent in each role.

For this deep-rooted sense of duty, fostered in me in early childhood, I am indebted to the Soviet ballet school and to the example, always before me, of my parents, indefatigable toilers of the ballet.

The Making Of A Ballerina

A dancer must be a hard plodder. Daily practice is his meat and drink and it must never cease, not even during summer holidays. I was still very young when I realized that airiness, beauty and inspiration in the dance can be achieved only through the greatest effort. I do not wish to sound pompous—I have never cared for high-flown phrases which, I think, fall short of expressing the true essence of our thoughts—yet, if we must explain what makes for the mastery and excellence of an artist, it is best to recall Gorky's words: talent is work. That is what he said, I believe.

Konstantin Sergeyevich Stanislavsky said practically the same thing over thirty years ago when he addressed a group of young actors of the Moscow Art Theatre before the opening night of *The Battle of Life*. "It may seem to the average spectator," he said, "that the prima ballerina's dancing in *Swan Lake* or *Don Quixote* is 'joy' rather than work. But little does he know how much attention, effort and actual *work* Yekaterine Geltser put in to *prepare* her famous *pas-de-deux* in these ballets, nor what she looks like in her dressing-room after the performance. Perspiration streams down her face and in her heart she reproaches herself for the least *nuance* she had failed to convey. . . . There is, of course, the 'joy of creation.' It does come to the real artist—but only after supreme effort in his chosen and dearly loved field when the *lofty aim* he sets himself is attained."

The words "lofty aim" (as well as a number of others) were underscored by Stanislavsky. To set oneself a lofty aim and to attain it—that is what gives meaning to art.

However, at the time I went to school it did not occur to anybody to discuss such matters with ballet dancers. Indeed, even after graduation we were left adrift where the more profound aspects of our art were concerned. Perform on the stage as you were taught at school! Work for technical excellence! Such was the simple credo of those days.

Of course, our work was not only physical—involving arms, legs and body. It was work of the intellect and heart as well. The intellect has its share in whatever the ballet dancer does. It is developed through the stimulation of not so much the theatre, music, librettos and choreographers, as of the environment that surrounds one beginning with one's childhood and school-days. The dancer will think independently, and boldly, will have broadness of vision only as he assimilates life's experiences, and as he masters the greatest of all sciences —the science of life. Of this significance of the knowledge and experience of life I shall speak later, when describing what I call my "coming of age school." But now whenever I think of my apprentice years they appear to me as one long period of plodding, work of the arms, legs and body—an everlasting grind at the *barre*.

However, it would be wrong and self-deceiving to say that I never grudged the time I spent in my youth and in later years over my eternal drills. I remember only too well the bright summer mornings during my holidays—I was then already grown-up and quite independent—when almost in tears I would approach the detested *barre*. I had a feeling as though a millstone were fixed about my neck. At that moment I hated the ballet, remembering with satisfaction that one of our poets had called it "that cruel art of ours." How I longed (especially if it was in summer and I lived on the shore of my beloved Lake Seliger) to drop what I was doing and follow my friends to the lake, climb into my canoe and paddle, paddle for all I was worth, over the shimmering expanse of the water, beneath the blue sky, and amid the rustling of the bulrushes. . . . But a hateful voice inside me kept whispering: "Work! Work! If you don't, you'll get nowhere, you'll be nothing but a *figurante*. . . . Work!"

Then a strange thing would happen. After only a few minutes of the drills I would feel the millstone lifting. A blessed relief would come over me. The thought that I had not shirked my duty, that I had resisted the temptation of going out and having a good time before my work was done, gave me a sense of satisfaction that bordered on vanity. And when the drills were done and I could call it a day I knew that I had earned my right to enjoy myself. It was good to get into the canoe, and catch up with my friends. . . .

This deeply-ingrained sense of duty in regard to my profession and my strict keeping to routine helped me to form a lifelong habit of working for improvement, which in many respects is responsible for the successes that have fallen to my lot.

When I graduated from ballet school my technique was still not of the order which, from a dictator, holding the dancer in perpetual dread of making a slip, becomes her helpmate, so trusty as never to obtrude either on herself or on the audience.

As I vaguely recall my graduation performance—I danced the lead in *Chopiniana*—and my *début* in the theatre as Princess Florina in *Sleeping Beauty*, so memorable to me, I must admit that technically and otherwise my dancing fell short of my expectations.

When I came on the stage I was seized by stage-fright which I suppose every dancer experiences on his *début.* What seemed good at the rehearsals fell flat at the performance. I danced, trying my best, but was being wafted away somewhere. My mind was a complete blank. I felt nothing, nothing except fear and a frantic anxiety to do everything just as I had been taught.

Even the leading ballet parts, such as Odette-Odelia in Chaikovsky's *Swan Lake,* which I was given at the age of eighteen, four months after my *début,* I danced without deeply understanding the characters I impersonated. This is true not just of my first year on the stage but for all of four or five years.

All those early years of my stage career were spent in falling into the swing of theatre life, in ridding myself of the habits and rhythm of the apprentice, in growing stronger in body and in acquiring the plastic poise and confidence which are so essential to the ballet dancer.

In discussing the plastic ideal which every artist must strive to attain, K. S. Stanislavsky wrote: "There are dancers and dramatic actors who have once and for all trained themselves to be plastic so that they need no longer think of that side of their physical movement.

The Making Of A Ballerina

Plastic movement has become second nature with them. Such dancers and actors do not dance, do not act, but move as is natural to them, and they cannot help doing it plastically."

This is the ideal and one must strive energetically all one's life to approach it. And if, as a result, plastic movement does not become second nature, it will at least be organic and natural, an integral part of one's stage habits. I do not know of such ballerinas or dancers who "need no longer give thought to that side of physical movement," actually to the technique of the dance. If there are such darlings of Terpsichore, I, alas, am not one of them. Whenever I dance, no matter what the ballet is, I am conscious of every movement I make, and the more difficult the dance is the more mindful I am of the technical details. Dancing Juliet for the hundredth or even the five-hundredth time I shall still not be able to perform the very difficult steps of the *adagios* in the first and second acts without preparing inwardly for them.

What is essential (as it seems to me) is to command technique with sufficient freedom to enable you to express the principal idea of the dance: the boundlessness of the feeling in Juliet's heart, the tremulous transports of Odette's love. Moreover, technical perfection should be such that the public should never notice, never suspect that any movement costs the dancer the least strain. The dance must flow smoothly in clear-cut, finely traced lines, like those which stamp the work of great graphic artists.

And indeed, the beauty and humaneness of the ballet

heroine's emotions cannot be expressed unless complete mastery of technique is achieved, not perhaps to the extent that the dancer "need no longer think of it" but at least so that her technique should not obtrude itself on the audience.

When, after five years of dancing in the theatre, I was cast as the Swan in Vaganova's version of *Swan Lake,* this role acquired special significance in my development as a dancer.

Dancing this part for many years, I was able to invest it with new meaning after my work on the role of Maria in Asafyiev's *The Fountain of Bakhchisarai.* This ballet (of which I shall speak later on in greater detail) made me realize much more broadly my potentialities as a dancer. It brought so much that was new to my problems in the dance, making them so much more "human," that I could no longer perform any of my other parts in the old way.

Masha in *The Nutcracker,* Aurora in *The Sleeping Beauty,* the Komsomol Girl in Shostakovich's *Golden Age,* Raymonde, Solveig in Grieg's *Ice-Maiden* and the Tsar-Maiden in *The Hump-Backed Horse*—were the parts I had danced. Certainly, they were not insignificant, but most of them now appeared to me hopelessly flat and meaningless. The part of Odette-Odelia, on the other hand, I saw in a new light.

With the passage of years, I was not merely coming into my own professionally, I was storing up experiences of life, I was reflecting on ballet, on symphonic music and opera, particularly on Chaikovsky's music; I was

reading. All this led me to realize the deep meaning
that lay behind the image of the Swan. The music itself
now revealed a new significance to me. It was as though
I were hearing it for the first time. I discovered in it
new enchanting possibilities for the dance and was able
to capture more fully its poetry. I benefited immensely
by working with Vaganova, a hard taskmaster and a
never-satisfied artist, who endeavoured to give a new
interpretation of *Swan Lake*. The debt I owe to Vaganova is enormous, and for that alone (to say nothing
of her numberless other services to our ballet) I shall
ever retain grateful memories of her.

In this early period of my career, I was greatly in-
fluenced by my friendship with the Timme-Kachalovs—
noble-minded, open-hearted people, artists in the fullest
sense of the word.

We met in Yessentuki, where I had gone for a cure.
As a result of my very unromantic ailment of the time
I was often a victim of fatigue, I avoided darting, abrupt
movements; I seldom smiled, was disinclined to run or
jump. Besides, I was very shy by nature. Perhaps all this
is partially responsible for that soft fluidity of movement
and line which has often been held to my credit and
which—who knows?—may have taken its origin, not in
the spirit within, but in the bodily condition that
brought me to Yessentuki. However, since this little
town in the Caucasus threw me in company with such
wonderful people I can feel nothing but gratitude to it.

Yelizaveta Ivanovna Timme, an actress of the Leningrad Pushkin Drama Theatre, and her engineer hus-

band, Professor Kachalov, began by making fun of my ailment, and inviting me to spend the remaining weeks after the cure with them on Lake Seliger. Their infectious vitality, their cordiality and friendliness, were amazingly effective in bringing me back to health. There, on Lake Seliger, my new friends awakened in me a deeper appreciation of the beauty of nature, one of them even composed a mock poem to the effect that my canoe and I were as inseparable as sisters. I ate fresh bread and milk fresh from the cow, against the doctor's orders, and returned a new person, stronger in body, happier in mind, and more than ever eager for work.

After the theatre I would now often go straight to the Timme-Kachalov's, to find the house full of clever, witty people, always arguing about art. They loved art without self-conceit or affectation—as only those can love it for whom it is not a mere diversion but serious work to which they dedicate their entire lives. The place glowed with excitement and animation, and though the company invariably consisted of actors, painters and poets, there was not even a hint of Bohemian laxity, which, to my mind, only the hopelessly vulgar can couple with true art. The atmosphere in the cordial home of my friends was edifying, intellectual and chaste.

It was there that I made the acquaintance of some of our country's finest actors, writers and artists, among them Korchagina-Alexandrovskaya, Studentsov, Yuriev, Tolstoy, Pevtsov, Gorin-Goryainov and Vivien. Without the least air of superiority they taught me to appreciate more fully the beauty and import of the drama. And

though there were no lengthy discourses on Stanislavsky's "method," its essence was brought home to me and
I realized that the theatre's greatness hangs upon realistic
and vivid acting.

"Do not fail to see it," my friends would often say to
me of one or another play. And I would go docilely,
knowing that I shall be asked how it impressed me and
why just so, and that from the ensuing conversation I
shall learn a great deal that will prove of benefit to me
in my own field.

Yelizaveta Timme, herself an outstanding dramatic
actress, was an ardent lover of the ballet. Some of my
most cherished moments were those when I listened to
her honest, well-meant criticism of my performances, in
which she noted very tactfully where I had failed and
where I had succeeded.

There were many things I could not understand at
first. The reason for this was perhaps a too great reverence
for accepted choreographic canons and rules. When I
was told, "You should make your dancing more dramatic,
more expressive," I would ask: "But how can I do it?"
My friends would then proceed to tell me what went
on in the soul of the Swan, describing shades of feeling
I did not even suspect, or explaining why the last time
I danced Giselle I had left the audience unmoved.

"I can't dance any other way," I would reply, "I don't
know how to do what you ask of me. I wasn't taught to
do it." The answer would be: "Neither do we know.
You must find the way yourself. Watch the same emotions in the drama and think of how they can be trans-

63

lated into ballet."

At times things of this kind were said casually, and at times in the heat of general argument over scenic forms. And as I listened, eager to imbibe all that was said, or controvert it, if need be, it would seem to me that now at last I had grasped that which was most important to me as an artist. And indeed I was beginning to understand that there is but one great truth underlying all scenic art: like the actor the dancer must delve deeply into the character that is to be portrayed, capture its very substance, and subordinate everything else to that. I came to realize that no matter how perfect the outer delineation of the role, the portrait will be lifeless and trivial unless it is invested with inner meaning.

However, when it comes to characterization, the dramatic actor has an easier time of it; he has language at his disposal, often the text of a genius. We ballet dancers have nothing but the music and mute movement. Hence we must learn to translate thoughts into movement, and endow the dance with the force of spoken words.

How can it be done? Not a single book on the ballet, not a single dancer gives an answer to this question. There have indeed been dancers who succeeded in making their art as expressive as the spoken word. Alexander Pushkin in his *Eugene Onegin* immortalized the name of Yevdokia Istomina, surely not because "in mid-air she beats her feet together," but because this "Russian Terpsichore" shows the "soul's soaring flight," because she brought a deep significance to her dance.

The Making Of A Ballerina

Maria Taglioni, Anna Pavlova, as well as many of the Russian ballerinas I was fortunate enough to see on the stage, and whom I strove to emulate, were great because they were able to invest their dance with profound meaning and with noble, edifying sentiment, to capture the mood and beauty of the music. Their dance carried the appeal of great poetry. How were they able to achieve this, and how were we to achieve it?

No one could give me an answer to this question. There are no set rules for dancing of this kind, I am afraid. True, we have a stock of movements which may be likened to the letters of the alphabet. With their help we form the "words" and "sentences" of our dance. However, the alphabet of real language may serve one to compose lovely poetry and another, doggerel. . . . And just as there are no set rules for good poetry, so there are no set rules for imbuing the mute but sublime art of the dance with great and noble meaning, of making it vivid and lucid.

The poet, it goes without saying, must be a master of words: he must know their every *nuance,* their subtle power of suggestion. Likewise the ballet artist must be well versed in the art of movement. However, for the poet, a perfect command of language is merely a preliminary condition in his creative work; just so for the dancer a perfect command of dance technique, or dance "alphabet" is only a preliminary condition to that which turns the "routine" of dancing into an art, and what is that?

Many years afterwards, when I read the concluding

lines of Stanislavsky's *The Actor Prepares,* this question was partly answered. "Singers must practise their scales," he wrote, "dancers their exercises, and actors train and drill according to the 'method.' Set your mind on this, make it a daily practice, learn to know your own nature, discipline it, and given talent, you shall develop into a great artist."

"Given talent. . . ." And talent is work. A vicious circle? I do not think so. Talent is work, true enough, but it is not only work as such, the actual performance of it, but the *ability* to work, plus an inordinate love for work, an *inner need* for it. Moreover, to this must be added the ability to feel, to think, to learn from books as well as from contact with people in all walks of life, to get at the bottom of people's characters, and perceive that which is essentially human and fine in them. To this must also be added the ability to observe life, to accumulate life's experiences and draw on their store for one's art; and also a something else for the explanation and definition of which we have not yet found the precise words but which nevertheless is tangible and exists objectively. Nor do I deplore the fact that this "something" evades us, and cannot be reduced to a mathematical formula. And if one day it is, it will not affect the number of talents in any way.

To me it seems every person has talent. It is only a matter of discovering that talent in time and guiding it in the proper way. . . . As time goes on more and more talents will come into their own in all spheres of endeavour, including the ballet, of course. Things are heading in that direction.

I do not think I am digressing from the main trend of my story, from what had induced me to reflect on my art, to express it through the media of thought and feeling. In the thirties, the period I am describing, I was still groping and the above ideas were still pretty vague in my mind. Yet it was precisely at that time, two decades ago, under the stimulating influence of the life around me—to which I was beginning to develop a more thoughtful and a more conscious approach—and under the influence of the Soviet art world, that I was acquiring the faculty of thinking over the meaning behind my parts. And it is this that helped me make my art worthy of the name.

At times the conversation and arguments at the Timme-Kachalovs' would go on to the small hours of the morning. One spring night, I remember, after an evening at the Timmes', I was taken by the actor Y. M. Yuriev for a walk through the city. It had seemed to me then that I knew Leningrad pretty well. But as I listened to Yuriev's quiet, fascinating narrative and was carried away by it, I realized at once how wrong I was and it made me reflect on the relativeness of human knowledge in general.

I couldn't imagine anybody knowing St. Petersburg, Petrograd and Leningrad better than this great actor. We walked through streets, which in the spurious twilight of Leningrad's "white nights" looked strangely airy and fantastic, and each house, as my companion spoke of it, seemed to breathe and live a life of its own.

Now it would be an assembly hall which saw the making of Russia's history, now rooms housing a collection of valuable statuary, or the seat of the one-time Freemason's Lodge, a garden with the world's most exotic blossoms growing in it, or a house once frequented by Pushkin.

The fullness and versatility of Soviet life, the discussions and contacts I made at the Timme-Kachalovs', close association with great and exacting Soviet artists —everything together constituted what I term my "coming of age school," which brought me within range of the theatre's broadest interests and profoundest ideals; the years I had spent in getting my choreographic training and the first five years in the theatre I call my "apprenticeship." It was the best school an artist could wish for; life itself, the accomplishments I witnessed daily in the ballet and the drama, my friendships with really talented people enriched me beyond measure, suggesting a new interpretation of the Swan and Giselle, and preparing me to tackle the still more exacting tasks in the roles of Juliet and Tao Hoa.

In the early months of my acquaintance with the Timme-Kachalovs, I was rehearsing *Swan Lake,* and everything around me seemed coloured by that work. Whatever I read, saw and heard came to me through the magic prism of that ballet and my problems connected with it. Odette occupied my thoughts. To me she was the essence of all that was feminine, tender and noble in woman. How could I best express these qualities?

It must be mentioned here that in the production I

68

was rehearsing, the part of Odette-Odelia was separated into two roles: Odette, the fairy Swan, and Odelia, real and diabolical. I was to dance Odette. According to the new libretto as well as the choreographical concept, Odette was truly a swan, whom Siegfried imagined to be a maiden. Hence I needed to find movements suited now to a real swan now to an imaginary maid.

It was not so much a matter of the technique of these movements, though they were difficult enough. I wanted to make my Swan reveal the torments of her soul, the tremulousness, the half-realized raptures of first love, its sanctity, utter devotion and power. I doubt whether I would have succeeded in conveying this had it not been for the advantages of "my coming of age school," for all I had learned in the home of the Timme-Kachalovs, in the circle of friends who were heart and soul in the life of the young Soviet theatrical culture, sharing in its successes, growth, joys and sorrows.

Soviet choreography, as it evolved, guided the ballet on towards greater depth and a wider range of themes. Our choreography and the great mass audience it now gained, an audience which was making the most exacting demands on the theatre imperiously called for portrayals of greater significance. We advanced through trial and error, through search and failure, from the ultra-revolutionary *Red Whirlwinds* and the ultra-industrial *Bolt* towards new poetic and realistic performances. For the first time great literature and new revolutionary themes found their way to the ballet stage— Pushkin's *Fountain Bakhchisarai*, Balzac's *Lost Illu-*

sions, The Red Poppy, and *Flame of Paris.* In my own case I cannot over-estimate the importance of Pushkin and his *Fountain of Bakhchisarai.*

Before the appearance of the new Soviet ballets (I have in mind the best ones, of which there have been and are no small number, and of which there will be more in the future) ballet music, excepting the beautiful scores in many of the classic operas and ballet of Chaikovsky, Glazunov and several West-European composers, was written with the sole object of helping the dancing and marking the rhythmic accents. It was required to be "dance music," easy for the ballerina to follow. No doubt, it is extremely important for ballet music to lend itself well to dancing. But if it is merely that the ballet might as well abandon the idea of re-creating the life of the human spirit on the stage. And to fail to do this would mean to strip of thought and inner emotion our ballet heroes and heroines, and to leave our Soviet audience unmoved. No matter how brilliant a performance is, if it is mere entertainment, if it is devoid of ideas, it will never satisfy the Soviet spectator.

Thus, the beautiful, elegant form of the classic dance had to be invested with new *content*—this is how we understood the demand of our audience. This became clear to us as far back as two decades ago when through a period of searchings, of failure and success, Soviet choreography came into its own.

In their earnest desire to realize the ballet's great possibilities, Soviet ballet-masters and dancers made music their starting-point. They discarded the old me-

thod of adapting the music to a stock of "dazzling"
dances and began to proceed from the very idea of the
music in moulding the pattern of the dance. This in
itself made for deeper content and put before the dancer
serious problems arising from the musical characteriza-
tions.

Thus a new chapter opened in ballet music. In it was
achieved a cohesion of action and thought, which made
the dance not only dynamic but replete with meaning.
Dances were no longer staged becouse the tune of a *waltz*
or *gallop* was "charming" but to express music with a
strong and significant appeal.

The new music could overstep the bounds of the
world of fantasy and depict the world of real people
and living passions. Boris Asafyev succeeded in doing
this in his music for *The Fountain of Bakhchisarai*.
With its clearly delineated musical portraits of Maria,
Zarema and Khan Girei, its forceful score, profound and
at the same time well adapted to dancing, this ballet
struck a new note, showing the backdoor to nymphs and
dryads, charming creatures, no doubt, but by no means
thinking ones.

Although the old Russian classical ballet presented in
the main fairies and princesses with their sparkling
variations, it, of course, was not altogether devoid of
thought, soul and idea. This is true particularly of ballets in which great dancers performed, they brought
fame to our ballet not only by their peerless technique
but by their highly inspired art as well. Still, it was the
ballerina who was technically brilliant, who could

"dazzle," that was the dominant figure in the old Imperial ballet. Nymphs and dryads, by their shallowness, helped to stifle thought and real human feeling on the ballet stage.

The Soviet era has made men and women take their rightful place as heroes and heroines of the ballet. This, of course, added immeasurably to the complexity of choreographic problems. But cannot the same be said of all the problems of our age, are they not exceedingly complex, profound and interesting?

The new ideas brought by the Soviet age were gaining a firm foothold in what is perhaps one of the most conservative arts. "Everything is in man and everything for man!"—this underlying idea of Soviet humanism, the idea of boundless faith in man, in his power, beauty and will to fight for happiness, became the motto of the new Soviet ballet.

Formerly the idiom of the ballet was not merely conventional (that it still is and will remain) but often utterly impotent; the dance itself as a rule was not able to express anything without the help of mime. There would be a constant alternation of mime and dance to make clear the meaning of the ballet. I think it significant that it was by drawing on the realism of Pushkin, the singer of Man, that we managed to break with this routine more effectively than in our attempts to do so in the new productions of old ballets. And from this point of view, it seems to me, *The Fountain of Bakhchisarai*, produced in 1934 by the Leningrad Academic Theatre of Opera and Ballet, was a landmark in the development of Soviet choreography.

When this ballet was rehearsed the choreographer, R. V. Zakharov, and we of the cast tried to get at the bottom of the relationships between the fascinating characters depicted in Pushkin's poem. Without doing this it would be utterly impossible to re-recreate them, and bring out the idea of the poem. Ballet dances of a general character that can be transplanted from one ballet to another, with nothing required but a change of costume, could never do for Pushkin. To interpret Pushkin the dance must be individualized, it must express only that which is intrinsically peculiar to the character of Maria or to Zarema, as the case may be, filled with gentle grief for the one, and with flaming jealousy for the other. The pattern may be woven of movements of flowing liquid grace, or flashing passion, depending on the character's state of mind at the moment.

In the "dialogue" between Maria and Zarema, the problem of "explaining" the feelings of the two women was thus solved without resorting to pantomine—the dance expressed everything. In the same way Maria's scene with Khan Girei, and the scenes in which she recalls her native land and her dear ones, as well as Zarema's dances, were all rendered comprehensive in the "action" of pure dance.

Maria is a part I keep working on all the time. This is also true of my other favorite roles. To the traits that I have found in the Swan and Giselle, Maria has added great humaneness and living texture. And whereas in my early portrayal of Maria an all-pervading grief was the dominant note, in later years the portrait changed, as though come to full-blown life. My pattern grew more intricate, brighter in color, revealing many new facets to the character. Thus, into the color scheme came tints of joy, youth, vivacity—in the dances of the first act. I love the part of Maria because the music and the dance express Pushkin's poetry so well, and as a result the ballet is subtle and stirring.

Pushkin's Maria, as I have already said, has made me revise a good deal in my previous roles. This is true, for example, of my Giselle. In Giselle I was faced with the problem of portraying love, hopeful and radiant in the first act, and tragic in the second, but in both acts so vital and powerful that it is able to conquer Myrta's evil will and even death itself. Herein lies the significance of *Giselle;* the ballet is not merely a repetition of the old story of a simple maid's seduction by a wealthy noble (those who think so err on the vulgar side).

In rehearsing *Giselle* I tried to conjure up the image of a "simple maid," I sought instinctively, as I had done in Maria and in all my roles since, for that something, that "magic word," if you like, to turn me into Giselle, to make me live her tragedy, and believe in it so utterly as to make the public believe in it too.

The new significance which I read into my roles brought me closer to Juliet.

As in Maria, in Juliet I proceeded from the music. Soviet composers have made an invaluable contribution to the ballet—they have given it music with meaning

and idea. And in moulding the pattern of our dance in
Romeo and Juliet we were guided by the melodies of
the music which revealed the spiritual world of our
characters.

Prokofiev's score in many place was abrupt, bewilder-
ing and "jarred" on the dancer. The frequent change of
rhythm was a decided handicap to the dancer, I remember when, after the first presentation of the ballet, the
dancers and all responsible for the production, including the composer, gathered, I could not refrain from
saying: "Never was a story of more woe than dancing
to Prokofiev's music, oh!" However this was merely a
jest; what I seriously thought was quite different: in
Romeo and Juliet, more fully than in *The Fountain
of Bakhachisarai,* there was harmony of thought and
action, and despite the new modern note it struck,
Prokofiev's music translated perfectly Shakespeare's
tragedy. To my mind that accounts for the ballet's great
success, for its undying loveliness.

When faced with the role of Juliet, fifteen years ago,
I thought it was beyond my powers to tackle it. Indeed,
the more I thought of the problems connected with the
part, the more formidable they seemed to me. In Juliet
I knew must be revealed an eternal human theme, a
theme of all time which Dante expressed in the line:
"Love, that denial takes from none beloved." The
atmosphere and the period, the feud between the Capu-
lets and the Montagues, were all of secondary importance, as compared to that great theme.

Among all nationalities we find extant legends and

poems telling the sad story of true love in conflict with circumstances, which, yet, are powerless to crush and destroy it. Such are Romeo and Juliet, Farkhad and Shirin, Tristan and Isolde. The theme is the same. Our problem was to give it Shakespearean amplitude. Where were we to find the power to do this? In hard work.

Shakespeare's portrait of Juliet is extremely concrete; it was important that in the ballet she should lose none of her Shakespearean color. Shakespeare's text itself suggested to me the carefree gayety of the early scenes, the flutter and agitation of the masque, the rapture of the balcony scene, the chastity of the marriage scene, the courageous overcoming of the fear of the tomb. . . .The outer image I sought in the portraits of the Renaissance, notably in the women of Botticelli's Primavera—Spring —is not that Juliet herself?

Prokofiev's score, dramatic, sensitive, close to the modern heart and at the same time consonant with Shakespeare, was a real inspiration. We had but to follow it in every movement to mould our dance into plastic forms, provided we made the most of the ballet "alphabet," inadequate though it is. Lavrovsky, the choreographer, sought to express perfectly the music and with it the great content of Shakespeare's tragedy.

It was not without a good deal of experimenting, however, that *Romeo and Juliet* was produced. And I must say here that in recent years we had begun to realize more and more the ballet dancer's dramatic potentialities, and acquired valuable experience along these lines. This is to some measure responsible for our boldness in undertaking to translate into ballet what is one of Shakespeare's greatest plays.

A play of all time, it lives on the stage, expanding in significance, gaining in meaning with every age. Shakespeare is so profound that we are ever discovering new possibilities in him. Thus, when several years after the Leningrad production, I began to rehearse Juliet in the Bolshoi Theatre in Moscow, where Prokofiev's ballet was being revived, I saw quite a different Juliet. I perceived her illumined by all of my life's experiences, by the years of war and victory.

More than ever Juliet appeared to me now as a character of strong will, ready to fight and die for happiness. This made me impart, for example, a new and more powerful dramatic quality to the scene in which Juliet defies her father and refuses to marry Paris whom she does not love; I tried to express in my dance Juliet's resolve, her defiant and courageous spirit. To me the new Juliet was possessed of moral fibre which under different circumstances would make of her a heroine ready to die for a patriotic cause, one close to us in spirit. Our great idea was to imbue this tragedy written four hundred years ago with the force of a contemporary theme and make it ring new. In that sense *Romeo and Juliet* was a *new* ballet.

And here I must make a reservation. While I greatly favor present-day themes, new ballet does not necessarily presuppose a contemporary setting and a modern theme. The modern theme in ballet is a problem which we are tackling now; but it cannot be solved easily and

77

simply. By new art, as well as by new ballet, we mean all that is consonant with our world outlook and our aspirations, all that assists us in our struggle and brings us closer to our great goals. That is why Pushkin, Beethoven, Shakespeare and Leonardo da Vinci are so near and dear to us. That is why we claim that the range of themes and subjects for the ballet has broadened immensely: from the battles of the Civil War, and the gallantry of the young people who fought in it, to the revolt of Spartacus, the Roman gladiator, from the struggle for peace in Italy to the philosophic poems of Nizami. All this can now be rendered by the new choreography and is already being shown on our stage.

Thus when we were staging *Romeo and Juliet* in Mosscow, to us, possessing the heightened sensibility that came of the war and its sufferings, it was a ballet steeped in our own age.

An actor lives, stores up impressions and experiences, little thinking that they may prove some day of great value in his work and even in some concrete role. But when he is given a role particularly suited to his temperament, and in which he can best realize himself as an artist, he "suddenly" feels that the whole course of his previous existence was, as it were, one long preparation for that role. All his memories, encounters, conversations, and even his minor thoughts and observations, the books he has read, are thrown into sharp focus, sifted and crystallized, to shape that one role, which for the moment has blotted out everything else. This is what happened to me in regard to my Juliet,

78

a new Juliet now, her character enhanced by my own experiences in the war years.

However, it was not a matter of any direct connection between my war-time experiences and my dancing. But it was that I felt more than ever drawn close to the people, whose gallant performance on the home and battle fronts saved our honor, human dignity and possibility to work in our chosen fields, from being trampled in the dust. I saw how close-knit Soviet people were in their common cause. Their every deed spoke of their devotion to the Motherland. They were giving their all, spiritually and physically, to the war effort. The realization of all this led me to dance Juliet—my first post-war role—differently in the Moscow production. I now wished to put greater emphasis on such features in Juliet as moral courage and resolve.

During the war all Soviet artists tuned their life wholly to the life of the people, realizing the people's keen need for them.

The cannon roared but the muses were not silent. The theatre continued to edify and delight the people by its art. From our fighting men we received daily corroboration of how dear the theatre was to them. Like most actors and dancers, I was getting mail from the front. The men who wrote to me were strangers but they were dear as brothers because they were fighting gallantly and courageously to save our country, to save our culture and art.

Among my mail were letters from Leningrad's fighting men who had seen me dance in that city before the war and remembered the ballets in which I appeared. There was one letter in particular that impressed me deeply. I received it in Molotov where the Kirov Theatre carried on after evacuation. My correspondent, Alexei Dorogush, writing from a village just cleared of the fascists, said: "In one of the cottages we found a picture of you as Odette in *Swan Lake*. The picture has a few bullet holes but all the same the boys took it to their quarters and while we're having a lull the orderly's standing assignment is to place fresh flowers in front of it every day."

Of course such marks of attention were pleasant and touching from those who fought and faced death every minute, and yet could think of art and of the theatre. But there is another reason for my quoting the letter. It was one among many things that brought to me a greater awareness of the close ties existing between the Soviet artist and the people. It made me feel the great debt I owe to the Soviet fighting men, who are able to cherish the memory of a joy once received in the theatre.

At every concert, at every performance, we actors and dancers witness an almost reverential attitude towards art on the part of our Soviet audience. This is to me an everlasting source of inspiration and delight. And it is clear how hard the Soviet dancer and actor must work to live up to this attitude.

During the war most of our spectators at the Bolshoi Theatre were men in uniform. Even if they came to Moscow for no more than a day or two Soviet army men made it a point to go to the theatre. This was indicative of our Soviet people's and our army's great impulse for poetry and high culture, of the loftiness of the people's spirit How could this not give the artist food for thought, not urge one to create new art, to broaden and deepen one's previous interpretations? In Molotov, whenever we performed to army audiences we got the warmest reception imaginable from a very packed house. I remember dancing in Leningrad, in 1944, before an audience of wounded soldiers, on an improvised stage platform in the Anichkov Palace, and feeling greater elation than on the brilliantly illumined stage of the Bolshoi Theatre in Moscow.

It is not with a mind to showing a direct influence of the events of the war on some particular role of mine that I speak at length of those stirring and unforgettable years. I merely wish to point out that a crucial period in our history was able to suggest much that enriched and ennobled our art.

In the days of the war, I pondered perhaps more than in other times over the essence of contemporary art and how it could best dedicate itself to expressing the aspirations of the people, of all who worked and fought.

Life was fostering in me an even greater devotion to my people.

It had long been my ambition to dance Tao Hoa— Red Poppy—the heroine from whom the ballet takes its name. Tao Hoa is a true daughter of her people and it is a role of a heroic order, requiring, together with lyricism, the expression of valor and great courage.

New problems and new difficulties confronted me in

Tao Hoa. To show this brave heroine of fighting China, a tender-hearted and gallant Chinese girl, to our people, friend and brother of the Chinese people, was a responsible and difficult task indeed.

Spiritually I was prepared for Tao Hoa by my previous roles, notably by Juliet. But Tao Hoa dies for a future happiness, of which she has a clear vision and in which she believes. And although she lived in the twenties I wanted to impart to her certain features of Chinese girls of our own day. Tao Hoa as a character grows before our eyes. I tried to make that growth convincing and to show its logical consummation in the great sacrifice Tao Hoa makes of her life—for the sake of the people's cause.

Tao Hoa has made me want to attempt other heroic roles. I should like to test my powers as Joan of Arc, or our immortal war heroine Zoya Kosmodemyanskaya, as well as other strong women characters of classic and modern literature.

The very features that I sought for and found in the Swan, in Giselle, in Maria, in Juliet and Tao Hoa— poetry, chastity of spirit, courage, faith in man, in man's reason and will to do good—are inherent in the new person born of the Soviet age. A champion of peace and justice, the new Soviet citizen has a noble and big heart. He is modest and selflessly devoted to his Homeland. He is the new man we meet and see everywhere and the qualities he possesses must be portrayed in contemporary ballet if we wish to do justice to our age.

However, this is no easy matter. But ballet, in general, is hard work. So is producing anything—growing grain, making machines, writing poetry. There can be no art unless one gives it a lifetime of toil and devotion, even more, for if one possessed two lives—to paraphrase Pavlov, the eminent Russian physiologist—and gave them both wholly to art, one would still not be giving enough.

I think it is in this spirit that all Soviet artists work and it is in this spirit that the composer, the librettist, the choreographer and the ballet dancer are to-day earnestly cooperating and using all the means at their disposal to produce new ballets that will be a glory to the Soviet age.

Yuri Slonimsky

INSIDE THE
BOLSHOI BALLET

A Little History

In 1773 THE TRUSTEESHIP COUNCIL of the Moscow Orphanage decided to set up a ballet class for its inmates. By then Muscovites were familiar with Ballet, and the Opera and Ballet Theatre was preparing to open its doors.

Filippo Beccari, a former dancer of the St. Petersburg Court Theatre, offered his services as an instructor. The Trusteeship Council, however, was sceptical of his ability to turn the little orphans into expert dancers. To show that he could do it, Beccari was willing to wait for his salary until his pupils became full-fledged dancers, asking to be paid at the end of a one-year course 250 rubles for each solo dancer and 150 for those who would show perfect precision in dance steps and prove themselves in pantomime ballet. There were many who wanted to learn dancing, and the result was beyond even Beccari's expectations: of 62 pupils, 24 became soloists.

The Orphanage thus became the cradle of ballet training in Moscow, supplying dancers to its permanent Ballet Theatre.

The Moscow theatre thrived because at the beginning it was free from Court tutelage, catered to audiences that were more democratic than those in the capital and employed many actors from among former serfs. It had distinctive features, which were reflected in its original repertoire and the peculiarities of its performance.

It was here, at the turn of the 19th century, that a new genre came into being—one inspired by the national comic opera—dance scenes suggested by folk festivals, games, Yule-tide and Shrovetide carnivals, etc. These dances were first staged by Vasily Balashow, a former inmate of the Orphanage and choreographer of the Petrovsky Theatre.

In 1837 St. Petersburg ballet-goers witnessed the Russian début of Maria Taglioni, while ballet lovers in Moscow were introduced to Yekaterina Sankovskaya, justly called the Russian Taglioni. Belinsky and Herzen called her the favorite of the students, while the writer Saltykov-Shchedrin said she was a herald of truth, beauty and goodness. These words described one of the major principles of Russian aesthetics in the classical dance, for a ballet character is splendid only when it reflects beauty of thought, feeling and deed. Sankovskaya personified spiritual purity and moral staunchness, and the Moscow audiences loved her for it.

Chance willed it that in her old age she should become the first teacher of the famous Stanislavsky.

Saltykov-Shchedrin said that, more than a ballerina, she was a plastic interpreter of a new word. On the Russian stage this new word was romanticism, which reached its peak in the 1830's. Deeper interest in man's inner life—in his psychology and emotions—and especially in lyricism brought about a reform in art. The

88

genre *scénes de la vie privée* gave way to romantic legends and fairy-tales dealing chiefly with the vicissitudes of woman's destiny.

This new, primarily lyrical content gave rise to an impetuous development of corresponding means of expression, especially in the case of the female dance. The technique of dancing *sur les pointes,* the multitude of leaps, *arabesque* and attitude poses in "flight," together with the old *terre-à-terre* dancing, helped choreographers to render the true feelings of their romantic heroes and heroines. Pantomime ballets, in which the dance served only as a link between mimic scenes, gave way to dance suites in which pantomime played the role of "conjunctive tissue" and the dance became the main thing. The way to romantic reform in the dance was paved by Didelot's *Zéphyre et Flore* (1808).

Russian ballerinas began to tour Western Europe in the 1830's, scoring one triumph after another. The first to go abroad was Sankovskaia. Zina Richard, was a ballet teacher at the Paris Grand Opéra.

The 1860's saw a new stage of Russian art, the movement for emancipation breathing new life into all its spheres, Ballet included. In 1869 Petipa staged *Don Quixote* (for which he himself wrote the book and Minkus the music). Revived by Alexander Gorsky in 1902, this ballet is still part of the Bolshoi repertoire.

It was at the Bolshoi and its ballet school that the renowned choreographer and teacher Carlo Blasis worked for three years (1861-64). Many of his Moscow pupils became teachers themselves and passed on to their pupils certain peculiarities of his classical school.

The glorious melancholy of the melodies of Chaikovsky's *Swan Lake* first rang out at the Bolshoi on February 20, 1877. Conservative critics misunderstood his music and claimed that it was poor in melody. The first producer, Julius Reisinger, failed to translate the score properly into stage characters. Another ballet master, Hansen, tried hard to breathe life into the ballet, but he was just as unsuccessful. And it was only some twenty years later that Lev Ivanov created through the dance a lyrical image of the swan and made *Swan Lake* the brilliant success it has been ever since.

Chaikovsky achieved what the best of his predecessors had striven for. He made Ballet, in terms of ideas and characters, a legitimate branch of the musical theatre. Ballet music became the most faithful servant of the dance and at the same time its real master. It could now be "plastically felt" and "visionally heard," irrespective of whether one was seeing the ballet or just listening to the music.

The enchanting music of *Swan Lake* and its poetic and inspired images were expressive of noble feelings which, in their turn, inspired the classical dance. Chaikovsky had "humanized" the dance. New horizons opened before Ballet. The stage dance was entering a new era.

* * *

A Little History

The 1890's were golden years for Ballet—within ten years the audiences saw three ballets by Chaikovsky, three by Glazunov, Borodin's *Polovtsian Dance,* Driga's *Arléquinade* and Arensky's *Egyptian Nights,* as well as dances scenes to Glinka's *Waltz Fantasy,* Liszt's *Second Rhapsody* and Chopin's piano pieces.

It was in these years that Petipa and Ivanov were at the peak of their fame, that Alexander Gorsky was making himself a name as a ballet master and Mikhail Fokine, later an outstanding ballet master, was first attracting attention. And it was in these years that the world was given a galaxy of splendid Russian ballerinas, headed by Anna Pavlova.

At that time the first books on Ballet were written and a ballet practice programme worked out. Vladimir Stepanov suggested a splendid system of notation which later enabled theatres the world over to re-create the ballets produced in Russia.

The turn of the century marked a new phase in the history of Moscow Ballet thanks to the opening of the Mamontov Opera House—the theatre which gave the world Fyodor Chaliapin—and the founding of the Stanislavsky and Nemirovich-Danchenko Art Theatre. This phase was characterized by an intense search for new directions and by a struggle against routine, and it was this and the influence of the Art Theatre that helped Gorsky, then a young ballet master and teacher, to develop his artistic world outlook.

In 1899-1901 he revived *The Sleeping Beauty, Raymonda* and *Swan Lake* and then modernized the old

91

ballet *Don Quixote, Pharaoh's Daughter, The Humpbacked Horse, Esmeralda* and *The Corsair*. In the 1910's he was at the peak of his career.

For many years Gorsky had thought of staging Flaubert's *Salammbô*. He finally did it in 1910 (music by Andrei Arends, sets and costumes designed by Korovin). With this ballet and with *Gudula's Daughter*, staged somewhat earlier, he continued the traditional cooperation between the ballet theatre and classical literature, making full use of choreography to depict the characters and the essence of the dramatic conflict of the novel. *Salammbô* was followed by Grieg's *Love Is Fast*, imbued with the spirit of folk life, and the first experimental translation of a symphony—Glazunov's *Fifth Symphony*—into ballet terms.

Gorsky proclaimed "harmony of components" the basic law of a dance drama. The artist and the musician, the dramatist and the choreographer, the actor and the producer, he said, should serve the same cause—rendering the ideological and artistic content. It was their task, therefore, to seek jointly for the best way to present the new production.

All his life Gorsky fought against the elements of dress concert in which Ballet then abounded. He wanted the dancers to live their parts, saying that otherwise there could be no real ballet characters. He urged enhancement of expressive means, especially of the dance. Every production should have its own expressive language, he said. Everything must be subordinated to the creation of an image. His dances were packed with detail, with "local color," whether with the aid of the folk dance or merely gestures.

In his search for the new, Gorsky often went to extremes. Speaking of the early days of his own career, Stanislavsky said: "My search for new ways was rather disorderly. I would dash from one extreme to another, taking along what I had found." This could well apply to Gorsky. He keenly felt that it was no longer possible to create in the old way and this feeling determined his whole activity. "Art that does not create anything is doomed to death, to self-destruction," he would say. "You must create."

Gorsky's creative quest rallied the best actors of the Bolshoi. Among those who took part in his productions were remarkable ballerinas such as Lyubov Roslavleva, Yekaterina Geltser and Adelina Juri, all of whom started their careers in the 1890's. Unfortunately, Roslavleva, an outstanding lyric dancer, died very early and Juri soon retired from the stage. The whole burden of the repertoire fell on Yekaterina Geltser and for thirty years she maintained the fame of Moscow Ballet. Having started with a brilliant success in *Raymonda,* she closed her glorious career with *Red Poppy,* the first Soviet ballet.

A few words about Vasily Tikhomirov, an outstanding dancer, actor and teacher, who worked well with Gorsky despite the fact that they disagreed on some points. Beautifully built, strong and possessing a perfect technique, he combined these qualities with excellent mimicry and plasticity. A connoisseur of old ballets, he jealously guarded and popularized them. As a ballet dancers owe him their training.

teacher, he trained more than one generation of ballet dancers, and many pre- and post-revolutionary Moscow

The ballets staged by Gorsky often featured Mikhail Mordkin, a wonderful dancer who was at home in whatever role he had to dance or play. He gave memorable performances as Mathô in *Salammbô*, as the charming and genial Basilio in *Don Quixote*, the emotional Prince in *Swan Lake* and the happy-go-lucky fisherman in *Love Is Fast*.

The lively, emotional expression of Mordkin and the austere, sculptural majesty of Tikhomirov were characteristic of the Moscow school of the male dance.

Like their Petersburg compatriots, Moscow dancers made many a triumphant tour abroad. The names of Sophia Fyodorova, Vera Koralli, Maria Reizen, Leonid Massine, Vyacheslav Svoboda, Vladimir Ryabtsey—pupils of Tikhomirov, Gorsky and other famous teachers of the day—were well known in other countries before the Revolution.

On the eve of the Revolution, however, there was a decline in Russian Ballet. There were much fewer new productions. Gorsky and Fokine were repeating their old experiments more and more often. Many dancers left imperial theatres to tour the country or work for the films.

The Moscow Ballet School admitted no new pupils between 1906 and 1910. It resumed admission in 1911-12, but on a much smaller scale. In 1915 it stopped again.

A Little History

This was part of the general crisis that was spreading to all the spheres of art on the eve of World War One.

* * *

A new phase in Russian art began after the October Socialist Revolution. Even in the early years, though exhausted by four years of world war and three of civil, the country allocated part of its meagre budget to keep the theatres going. Their doors were opened to hundreds of thousands of new theatre-goers—workers, peasants and soldiers. Close fruitful contact was established between the theatre and the audiences.

The Moscow Ballet School resumed activity in 1920 on the new, broader basis of special and general subjects.

Most of the Moscow ballet veterans remained at their posts. Gorsky headed the ballet company of the Bolshoi until his death in 1924, while Arends, one of the country's oldest conductors and ballet composers, was in charge of its orchestra. He was succeeded by Yury Fayer, whose 40 years as a Bolshoi Theatre conductor were recently celebrated in Moscow.

In the early 1920's the Bolshoi ballet company was joined by Asof Messerer, Igor Moiseyev and Mikhail Gabovich, all of whom later became prominent figures in Soviet ballet.

Extremely gifted and possessing perfect technique, Messerer was equally at home in any dance—eccentric, grotesque, character or rigidly academic. The ease of his leaps and the perfection of his classical lines were amazing. His repertoire included not only leading classical roles, but a number of dances he himself had created and perfected. At present he is in charge of a higher ballet school and produces ballets.

Moiseyev began his career as a character dancer, but soon became a ballet master. Since 1937 he has headed a folk-dance ensemble and in this capacity he has revived a great many gems of folk dances. His personal experience has helped to establish many folk-dance ensembles in Soviet republics and abroad.

At first Soviet ballet producers and dancers were inclined to reject all that was old. They turned to experiments with all sorts of productions—"neo-classical" and "abstract" ballets, which consisted of formal patterns; rhythmical plastic calisthenics; buffoonery turned into dances;; mimic dramas; *tableux vivifiés;* acrobatic *études,* and dances called "machinery of a modern city."

Gifted choreographers like Kasyan Goleizovsky in Mosscow and Fyodor Lopukhov in Leningrad turned their talents to composing dances of the variety type.

In the 1920's Soviet Ballet went through all the phases of barefoot naturalism, strident constructivism, unnatural plastic expressionism and erotic orientalism.

But time and reality, as usual, exposed the fallacy of the conceptions then prevailing. They showed that all these formalistic innovations, denying as they did the role classics play in art, lead nowhere, while the classical heritage constitutes a reliable foundation for new creations. And as practice has proved, the audiences prefer classical Ballet to extravaganzas.

A Little History

On the tenth anniversary of the October Revolution, the Bolshoi staged Gliere's *Red Poppy*. There was much that was naive in theme, music and production, and yet *Red Poppy* scored an unparalleled success and was presented 200 times in two seasons. *Red Poppy* is prominent in the history of the Soviet Ballet as the first successful attempt to render a modern theme on the ballet stage, as an unprecedented presentation of the theme of the movement for national liberation.

Gradually the Bolshoi became the musical and choreographic centre of the country. This made it necessary to expand its ballet company, to reinforce it with young talent and to enlist the assistance of the best teachers. That explains the transfer to Moscow, in the late twenties. and early thirties, of a group of Leningrad dancers. Worthy of special mention among these new-comers is. Olga Lepeshinskaya, who made her Bolshoi Theatre début in 1933.

Vigorous leaps, excellent steadiness *sur les pointes, développée,* exceptional ability to perform intricate steps. (especially *pirouettes),* the ease with which she danced, her humor and histrionic gifts have gained Lepeshinskaya wide popularity. The feeling of contemporaneity helped her to portray the modern girl—lively, gay, full of initiative.

* * *

Soviet Ballet made great progress in the thirties. These were the years of new ballets that have since become Soviet classics, years which produced outstanding performers, ballet masters, musicians, script writers, critics and designers. Ballet performances were enriched with new contents, and new genres were developed; means of expression were extended and direction enhanced.

Th Bolshoi continued to improve its Ballet. Its repertoire was increased to include some excellent new productions: *Flame of Paris* (music by Asafiev, book by Volkov and Dmitriev, choreographer Vainonen), which tells of the heroism of the French revolutionaries of 1789. Pushkin's romantic poems *The Fountain of Bakhchisarai* and *The Prisoner in the Caucasus* (music by Asafiev, book by Volkov, ballet master Zakharov) ; Yury Olesha's fairy-tale *Three Fat Men* (music by Oransky, book and choreography by I. Moiseyev); Gogol's patriotic epic *Taras Bulba* (music by Solovyov-Sedoi, book by Kaplan, ballet master Zakharov). Ballets on modern themes began to play a big part in the Bolshoi repertoire. Two new modern ballets—*The Baby Stork* and *Svetlana* (music by Klebanov)—were successfully staged at the Bolshoi by Radunsky, Popko and Pospekhin. *The Baby Stork,* a simple tale of Soviet children, is still part of the Soviet ballet repertoire.

The years of the Great Patriotic War, when the Nazi hordes invaded the country and were advancing on Moscow, Leningrad and the Volga, were years of severe trial for art. Soviet art belied the saying: "When the cannon roar, the muses are silent." True, there were fewer *premières,* but the ballet company worked with redoubled effort. The Bolshoi was evacuated to Kuibyshev, where it remained for three years and where it produced the new ballet *Crimson Sails* (music by Yurovsky, book by Grin, choreographers Radunsky, Popko and Pospekhin). A small group of dancers remained in Moscow performing at the Bolshoi Filial.

In 1940, the Bolshoi and its Filial presented 112 ballet performances. In 1942 the Bolshoi Filial alone gave 126 ballet performances and the main company in Kuibyshev gave another 89. The dancers were animated by patriotic enthusiasm: teams toured the front lines performing for the troops, many dancers joined the armed forces and others left for work in dance ensembles.

The post-war years at the Bolshoi were quite eventful, and one event is particularly noteworthy: Galina Ulanova joined the Bolshoi permanently.

Ulanova is the very embodiment of the Russian school of classical dance. A successor, of the best ballerinas, she has become our ideal lyrical and tragic dancer. Truth, simplicity in expressing the most complex emotions and humaneness of each movement and pose are some of her charming qualities. Ulanova does not go in for bravura as such, she does everything quietly, without any desire to show off. She does not act or dance, but lives the dance.

The simplest thing in the art of creation is sometimes the most difficult and that has been proved by Ulanova. Having achieved technical perfection, she knows how to conceal strain under an appearance of harmonious calm. She subordinates everything to one task—to breathe life into those steps that often seem superfluous and pointless. "Laconism," which has become Ulanova's mot-

to, is one of the commandments of the Russian school—
it was Anna Pavlova's motto too.

Soviet dancers deeply respect Stanislavsky's teaching.
They are united by the school of psychological realism,
to the development of which the founder of the Moscow
Art Theatre devoted all his life. Stanislavsky left us a
wise definition of two types of ballerinas—represen-
tatives of two types of dance. Some ballerinas, he said,
perform without being in the least concerned with the
contents of the dance, create forms that are devoid of
all essence and merely reproduce plastic movements.
Stanislavsky was highly critical of such ballerinas. They
cannot, he stressed, achieve the main thing—make the
invisible creative life visible.

But there are ballerinas of another type, who have
once and for all worked out a plastic technique that is
their second nature. These ballerinas, Stanislavsky
wrote, "do not dance, do not perform—they live."

We do not know whom Stanislavsky had in mind
when he was writing these lines—Pavlova, Roslavleva,
Geltser or someone else. But it fits Ulanova perfectly.

A ballet character is above all a dance character—
"coherent movements of the whole body," as Noverre
defined it. Stanislavsky, who said as much, held that
the main thing in a dance is its "melody," its unbroken
line of movements. The dance "melody" requires harmonious movement of all parts of the body, to the very
fingertips. And harmony gives birth to truthful art.

The visible "music" of Ulanova's dance appeals to

millions because through it she asserts the theme of noble love and heroic deeds, upholding her convictions as she "sings" them.

In Ulanova's interpretation, the ordinary feelings of joy or grief, thirst for happiness or disappointment, resolution or hesitation, become extraordinary, or rather extraordinarily beautiful. Like a girl from a fairy-tale she sheds tears of pearls. Her heroines are faithful not only to their hearts but also to their minds. And that is something new. With her the art of dancing is not just the poetry of a passionate heart—as it was with the best ballerinas in the past—but poetry of lofty thoughts as well. It is of her that scenarists, composers and choreographers think when they create a new ballet, and designers too, when they think of new settings and costumes.

All three of Prokofiev's recent ballets now seem to have been written expressly for Ulanova (Juliet, Cinderella, and Katerina in *The Stone Flower*). *The Fountain of Bakhchisarai*, in which Ulavona began her great career as the disconsolate and faithful Maria, is still as popular as ever.

The most outstanding of our younger dancers are Maria Plisetskaya and Raisa Struchkova. Their stage biographies are still short, but their gift reveals itself more vividly and improves with each new performance. They have brought much that is fresh and interesting to the gallery of characters created at the Bolshoi.

Maya Plisetskaya has already danced Odette and Odile, Zarema and Raymonda, Laurencia and Quiteria. This list of roles is an illustration of the scope of her mastery and skill. And to each role Plisetskaya gives a color all her own. The lines of her dance are most expressive. She is impetuous and the width of her leaps is so great that even the Bolshoi stage seems all too small.

Struchkova's dance is musical, graceful and elegant, and at the same time sincere and simple. Her creations breathe a youthful charm and warmth. Her excellent mimicry faithfully conveys her emotions. She can play vastly different roles. Some like her in comedy parts, others in lyrical-dramatic roles. But all agree that there is something very poetic in her stage portrayals. She has already danced Lise, Giselle, Cinderella, Maria and Juliet.

There are many ballerinas and *premier danseurs* who joined the Bolshoi only a few years ago. There are Nikolai Fadeyechev, a talented young dancer who shone as Siegfried and who is now rehearsing the role of Albert; Boris Khokhlov, who has confidently danced Siegfried, Désiré and other parts; Gennady Ledyakh, who scored as Basilio in *Don Quixote* and Frondoso in *Laurencia;* Nina Timofeyeva and Rimma Karelskaya, who vie with each other in their interpretation of Odette and Odile; Yaroslav Sekh, a talented character dancer who attracted attention by his performance as Mercutio; and Lesma Chadarain, who does both classical and character dances.

There are so many gifted young dancers at the Bolshoi and they are so different that it is simply impossible to give all of them the praise they deserve.

A Little History

The old Orphanage building still faces the Moskva River and the Kremlin. But there are no longer any orphans there, nor does it train dancers any more.

Now there is more than one ballet stage in the capital. The majestic Bolshoi Theatre stands in the centre of a beautiful square. Its choreographic school is nearby. A little distance away is the Bolshoi Filial and in the same street, a few hundred yards away, is the Stanislavsky and Nemirovich-Danchenko Musical Theatre, which presents original ballets.

The ballet company of the Bolshoi and its Filial is 221 strong. It has a reserve of more than 300 pupils. The choreographic school gives concerts and stages ballets which are very popular.

The Bolshoi Theatre stage is 26 metres deep, that is, 9 metres deeper than that of Covent Garden. To fill this stage with a crowd of Spanish peasants or citizens of Verona, you need a huge ensemble. For that reason the theatre employs many supers.

However, there is yet another participant in all these shows: the spectator, the most active and enthusiastic participant of all. Soviet society has not only prepared Ballet for the spectator, but also the spectator for Ballet. Every year more than 1,000,000 adults study choreography in various amateur theatrical groups. Several million children are taught ballet plastics and music. These people watch ballet productions from a professional point of view that is both critical and encouraging. These people are real balletomanes. There is no limit to their interest in the art of dancing.

Repertoire

THE OLDEST BALLET in the Bolshoi repertoire—778 seasons old—is Adam's *Giselle*, a wonderful creation of French genius. It has a very rare quality —a "harmony of components" that makes for a wonderful dramatic alloy. Chaikovsky called *Giselle* a poetic musical and dancing gem. In composing his works he read and reread the score of *Giselle*. In *Giselle*, music, book and dances form a single whole. It is a specimen of perfect continuity of action towards its climax. Its characters are simply yet expertly depicted. *Giselle's* naïve melodies blend with the emotional movements of its heroes; its purely choreographic plot is thoroughly consistent.

All the characters, all the important situations develop through the dance. The romanticism of the dance by the *corps de ballet* in the second act knows perhaps no equal. And all this serves one profound idea which always moves the spectator—that love is stronger than death.

Giselle disappeared from the theatres of the world for some 50 years after 1860 but was saved from oblivion by Russian Ballet, which raised this creation of Gautier, Saint-Georges, Perrot, Adam and Coralli to new heights. Generation after generation of choreographers and dancers enriched its dances and enhanced its content. Petipa, who had always admired *Giselle*, lovingly developed the elements of its dancing dramaturgy, while Fokine and Gorsky further revised it. In a word, the *Giselle* of today is very different from the Parisian *Giselle* of 1841.

In the Russian version the emphasis gradually shifted from the first act to the second. The main theme is no longer the tragedy of a maid seduced, as it was 100 years ago. The Wilis are no longer depicted as avengers, but as judges of honor. The heroes' love is tested at the fantastic gathering of the Wilis. They pass the test and win the sympathy of the audience.

The modernized *Giselle* has returned to the Paris Grand Opéra and is now included in the repertoires of most of the ballet theatres of the world. Soviet ballerinas have endowed Giselle with a thirst for happiness and this is reflected in the most tragic sequences of the ballet.

A special place among the ballets is occupied by *Don Quixote* (music by Ludvig Minkus). It was first staged 87 years ago at the Bolshoi. Since 1901 theatres have been staging the original Gorsky version of the ballet.

People always speak of *Don Quixote* with ironic condescension and this, indeed, is more than justified. The story of the Knight of the Rueful Countenance served the composer and the scenarist merely as a pretext to show some sequences that describe the humorous love adventures of the innkeeper's daughter and the barber. And yet, despite all criticisms, this ballet continues to live and rejoice spectators and performers, although they know very well that it is full of weaknesses. A choreographer of great imagination, Gorsky endowed the dances with such passion, color and rhythm that the audiences fall victim to their first impressions and ignore all the short-comings.

There is probably no other old ballet that contains such a festive blend of classical and character dances as does the first act of *Don Quixote*. The clever arrangement of mass and solo dances, classical and character, lyrical and comical, grotesque and ludicrous, make this old ballet a classic, at least the best parts of it.

It is not surprising, therefore, that its influence is as great as ever. The first act as staged by Gorsky has shown choreographers how to depict the people as the hero of a ballet.

The oldest of the Soviet ballets—*Red Poppy*—is now over 25 years old. In 1949 Lavrovsky revised it. *Flame of Paris* is only five years younger, but there is a bigger span between them in content and forms of expression.

Gliere's *Red Poppy*, laid in the China of the 1920's, tells of a Chinese actress who seeks her place in life. The people, whom she eventually joins, are in the background.

Asafiev's *Flame of Paris* shows France in the 1789 Revolution. It is also about an actress who, like the actress in *Red Poppy*, finds her place in the people's struggle for freedom. But the people here are in the foreground.

The third act is the most colorful. Here Asafiev revealed a new world of images—the dance and song of the "third estate" of the French revolutionary era. Their intonations required the ballet master Vasily Vainonen to create an original choreographic speech—striking, imbued with national humor, excitement, wrath and thirst for struggle. The choreographer created new plastic accents, sharp, springy movements, abrupt gestures of muscular arms. The dance grows into a powerful symbol. It is the spark that sets Paris aflame.

The best dances of this ballet show that the seemingly frozen *pas* of the classical dance are quite capable of taking on new elements and that a bold, imaginative choreographer can endow them with new content. They also show that there are no conflicts between classical and character dances if they both serve to create an image. It is not surprising that *Flame of Paris* remains a happy example of innovation for several generations of masters of Soviet ballet—both performers and choreographers.

On May 13, 1956, the Bolshoi Theatre gave the 300th presentation of *The Fountain of Bakhchisarai*. It was first staged in 1936. The Bolshoi ballet company had been experimenting with Pushkin's works for a whole century before it succeeded, before it became possible to speak of a real Pushkin ballet.

The Fountain of Bakhchisarai revives the genre of romantic poem in a new guise. The ballet reflects the poet's thought that love and violence are incompatible, that true love is all-conquering.

Pushkin showed the ballet theatre the way to interpret lofty thoughts. He was the first to teach dancers how to master new ideas and poetical resources.

The romantic form of expression, so peculiar to Pushkin's earlier works, accords well with the poetical nature of the art of dancing.

Perfect understanding by composer Asafiev of ballet dramaturgy, his skilful use of "speaking pauses" which we have inherited from the ballet music of the past, clear-cut ideological and artistic conception of the production and its theatrically—all this should be put to the credit of the music of *The Fountain of Bakhchisarai*. We highly esteem Asafiev for linking Soviet Ballet with classical literature—with Pushkin, Gogol and Balzac. He taught musicians how to interpret original literary works. And at the same time, through his scores, he gave composers and choreographers a series of lessons on correlations between the component parts of a ballet. Working with him younger ballet masters went through a whole course on poetic interpretation of ballet images. They also co-operated fruitfully with the dramatist Volkov, the author of many ballet books—from *Flame of Paris* to *Spartacus*. His book for *The Fountain of Bakhchisarai* is an excellent example of a ballet drama.

The Fountain of Bakhchisarai captivates the audiences by the psychological realism of its characters. This applies primarily to Girei through whom the poet (and after him the authors of the ballet) expressed his main idea.

In the first act Girei appears as an eastern potentate who is confident of his might, a magnificent beast, cruel and invulnerable. And then comes the first blow: he tears the vail from Maria's face and is struck by her beauty. He is surprised, enraptured. And seemingly against his own will he bows before the captive girl.

In the second act Girei behaves as one in a dream. His body and hands are limp, his gait is slow. His face is lifeless. When the orchestra strikes up Maria's sad and clear melody, a shade of a happy smile flits across his petrified face.

In the third act we see another Girei. He comes to Maria's room not as a soldier, a lord or a lover, but as a slave. He is utterly confused. In his *adagio* with Maria he now proudly offers her all his riches for her love, now falls at her feet, now embraces her with the timidity and passion of a youth but then quickly releases her, as if alarmed by his own transport.

And finally in the fourth act he appears as one who sees no reason to live after Maria's death. Nothing moves him, neither joys nor woes. The man in him has destroyed the beast in him.

The Fountain of Bakhchisarai has become a Soviet classic. It marked the beginning of Ulanova's brilliant career. It also brought fame to many dancers in Moscow and Leningrad: to Gusev and Smoltsov (Girei), Sergeyev and Gabovich (Waclaw), Messerer and Farmanyants (Nurali) and Vecheslova, Iordan, Shelest, Sulamith Messerer, Maria Sorokina, Maya Plisetskaya and Natalia Konyus (Zarema).

Quite different from *The Fountain of Bakhchisarai* is the ballet *Laurencia* (music by Alexander Krein, choreographer Vakhtang Chabukiani), so called after the heroine

of Lope de Vega's famous tragedy *Fuente Ovejuna.*
Laurencia, first produced at the Kirov Theatre in Leningrad in 1939, had its Bolshoi Theatre *première* this
season.

The Bronze Horseman belongs to the category of
monumental ballets. It was first produced in 1949, on
the 150th anniversary of Pushkin's birth.

The ballet is not equal to the poem. Pushkin's philosophical idea is there, but it is not made the main theme.
It is a sort of illustration of the famous poem, of
the beauty of St. Petersburg, of its white nights of which
Pushkin and Dostoyevsky wrote, of Pushkin's verse. It
would have been more correct to call the ballet *Yevgeny
and Parasha,* inasmuch as it deals chiefly with the
dramatic love of these two young people.

The mature master dancers of Soviet Ballet (such as
Gabovich, Yermolayev and Preobrazhensky) love this
hero, Yevgeny. Some of them depict him as a romantic
lover who has suffered misfortune, others as an op-
pressed and humiliated man who regards his love for
Parasha as the only justification of life, yet others present him as a naïve young man who loses his reason in a
moment of trial.

Gliere's music is an important part of the ballet. The
composer skillfully blends symphonic music and ballet
melodies. His music, dedicated to St. Petersburg, to
Peter I and the Bronze Horseman, is well known: it is
often rendered at symphony concerts, over the radio
and television.

Not since the days of *The Corsair* has the Bolshoi

Theatre seen such stirring scenes as the flood in *The Bronze Horseman*. The crowd rushes frantically about the Neva embankment as the waters overflow the river banks, inundate the square, foaming and raging around the buildings and the monument to Peter I. People perish in the waters; wreckages and boats float across the stage—the picture of a terrible flood is complete.

Yet most of the merits of the ballet, in my opinion, have little to do with the main thing—with the theme and its interpretation by the language of the dance.

Completely different in character and genre is the ballet *Mirandolina* (music by Sergei Vasilenko), first staged by the Bolshoi Theatre in 1949. *Mirandolina* captivates by its humor, lively comedy and variety of choreographic expression.

Vainonen, who produced the epic *Flame of Paris*, dedicated his composition to the talented players of the Bolshoi Theatre, to the dancers who performed in it. Lepeshinskaya (Mirandolina), Yermolayev (Ripafratta), Kondratov (Fabricio), and Radunsky (Count Albaforita) make the ballet a merry and diversified concert, leaving the spectator highly satisfied. The production has not become stale in the six years since its *première;* on the contrary, it becomes more colorful with each presentation.

Another ballet that has proved highly successful with Muscovites is *Shuraleh* (produced by Leonid Yakobson), which has been running at the Bolshoi Filial since 1955. It was first staged before the war at a theatre in Kazan, capital of the Tatar Republic. The talented young composer Yarullin did not live to see the success his first ballet has scored—he gave his life for his country in the war. In 1950 *Shuraleh* was produced by the Kirov Theatre in Leningrad and since then it has been included in the repertoires of many theatres the country over.

The secret of its success lies in its charming story, adapted from a fairytale by the Tatar classic Tukai, in its use of Tatar folklore, in the original music and excellent production.

Once upon a time in a dense forest there lived a goblin, or Shuraleh, in Tatar. The forest was the playground of girl-birds, who would shed their wings and play games. But the evil Shuraleh was an enemy of happiness and joy. One day he stole the wings of the Girl-Bird and prevented her from flying away with her friends. In the forest the Girl-Bird met the brave hunter Batyr. The young people fell in love and left for Batyr's village.

The second act shows the wedding. Shuraleh appears in the village and throws the wings to the Girl-Bird. She flies away and is dragged to the forest by the crows, sent by the goblin.

Batyr leaves to look for his beloved. The evil spirits in the forest, headed by Shuraleh himself, attack him. Unable to withstand their onslaught, he sets fire to the forest. The flames kill all the evil spirits, but Batyr himself is trapped. The Girl-Bird has wings and can save herself, but she refuses to do so. She wants to live and die with her beloved. And the flames retreat before love.

The young people are saved.

We have kept to the very end of this short review two ballets by Prokofiev—*Cinderella* and *Romeo and Juliet*.

The Bolshoi Theatre *premiére* of *Cinderella* took place in 1945, *Romeo and Juliet* was first staged the following year.

Prokofiev dedicated *Cinderella* to Chaikovsky, often saying that he meant it as a sort of sequel to *The Sleeping Beauty*. The music of *Cinderella* does resemble Chaikovsky's, but that does not make it any less Prokofiev's. On the contrary, writing it, the composer enriched himself, found something new. That new was the development of the philosophical beginnings of musical thinking and the enhancement of the lyrical and emotional aspects of music. In the score the leading role is played by the string instruments, something unusual for Prokofiev. Their cantilena reminds one of classical traditions and at the same time develops the composer's peculiar talents.

Chaikovsky inspired Prokofiev to write splendid waltzes. And that was new too, for there were very few waltzes in Prokofiev's earlier compositions.

Prokofiev, whose music was always quite forceful and at times sharply rhythmical, composed soft, lyrical melodies for *Cinderella*. Prokofiev's ability to ironize and depict grotesque characteristics enabled him to draw a vivid picture of the Court, of the evil stepmother and of the silly and selfish sisters of Cinderella.

The composer painted with great sympathy and love the image of Cinderella herself, bringing out her lofty spirit and noble heart. *Cinderella* shows how much Prokofiev owes to classical traditions. They opened new horizons before him and helped him to find what he had sought all his life—a positive hero.

There are ballets which bring success to all its creators —the script writer, musician, choreographer and artist. Some ballets owe their success to music, others to the dance. The brilliant music in *Cinderella* overshadows both the talented direction of Zakharov and the settings of that wonderful Soviet artist Pyotr Williams.

There is much in Zakharov's and Williams' work that is undoubtedly spectacular and striking. One needs only recall the scene at the ball when Cinderella hurries home as the clock strikes twelve. The moving decorations create the impression that the scene is changing. The Prince's round-the-world voyage in search of the owner of the glass slipper is made extremely colorful by the artist. Also memorable is the scene in which the walls of Cinderella's home part to reveal the changing seasons of the year.

Romeo and Juliet is an epoch-making phenomenon. It shows that Ballet has acquired new qualities without which it would have been impossible to present Shakespeare on the choreographic stage.

This ballet has already gained world-wide popularity. It has been popularized by symphony concerts, radio broadcasts, long-playing records and the ballet-film which, incidentally, is worse than the original stage production.

Choreographer Lavrovsky and artist Williams show a perfect example of fruitful co-operation. This ballet is

Repertoire

Lavrovsky's masterpiece.

For two whole centuries ballet masters and dancers, the world over dreamed of staging Shakespeare. We know of "the passionate pantomime" *Romeo and Juliet* staged by the Danish choreographer Galeotti. In 1809 *Romeo and Juliet* was presented on the St. Petersburg ballet stage (music by Steibelt, ballet master Valberkh). It was in those days, too, that Vigano, whom Stendhal lauded, composed his Shakespeare ballets. There were, too, a great many extravaganzas "adapted" from Shakespeare's plays, staged in Paris, Berlin, Vienna and Milan.

Indignant at the way the great playwright was being misinterpreted, Gogol wrote: "It is strange to see Shakespeare performed by dancers in kid-skin trousers. What is there in common between Shakespeare and these dancers? All they have is legs; he had a head" And Gogol was not alone in this opinion.

Chaikovsky, a great lover of Ballet and interpreter of Shakespeare in music, categorically refused to compose ballet music for *The Tempest*. "The story of *The Tempest* is too big and too deep for a ballet," he wrote to the man who was engaged on the book. "I simply cannot imagine Miranda or Ferdinand doing *battements, entrechats,* etc." Sad as this may sound, Chaikovsky was right: the ballet of those days could not have coped with Shakespeare's themes, for it did not possess the means to bring out his thoughts.

Let there be no mistake. The task is not merely to translate Shakespeare into the language of the dance. Such a vulgar understanding of the task can only lead

115

to ludicrous results. The task that has been bequeathed us by the classics of symphonic music and opera is immeasurably more complicated. One can faithfully present the story of the original and yet depart from the main thing—from its poetic truth. Faithfulness to Shakespeare is above all faithfulness to his ideas and images and not to the sequence of stage situations or their number in drama and Ballet. To achieve this faithfulness required a new approach, and this new approach was developed by Soviet Ballet in the process of staging Pushkin. Pushkin helped our Ballet to build up leading characters.

Noverre said that there could be only four leading characters in a ballet. Armed with Shakespeare's realistic method, the masters of Soviet Ballet have belied this canon of the dramaturgy of the past. In *Romeo and Juliet* we see not just the story of our heroes' love, but scenes of the morals and passions of a whole epoch. It was this interpretation of the tragedy (opera composers did not dare interpret it in this manner) that made it possible to bring out the main theme—the unequal struggle waged by the children of tomorrow against the injustice of yesterday.

Esthetics—
By Way of an Epilogue

T HE REPERTOIRE of the Bolshoi Theatre
shows a vast variety of themes, genres and styles. The
names associated with its Ballet include Petipa and
Gorsky, Lavrovsky and Zakharov, Chabukiani and
Fokine (his *Les Sylphides* has recently been revived),
Radunsky and Messerer, Vainonen and Goleizovsky (he
is the producer of the Polovtsian Dances).

The Bolshoi Theatre repertoire includes classical and
Soviet ballets. The organic interrelation between tradi-
tion and innovation constitutes the basic principle of
Soviet Ballet.   .

Our love for the classics was born and grew in an
atmosphere characterized by temptation and trial. We
have borne it through nihilism that denied the heritage
of "imperial" ballet in favor of a false "leftist" art that
is falsely understood, in favor of "innovation"; and
through fetishism that aimed at turning Ballet into a
collection of lifeless canons.

The question, of course, is not that of mechanically
accepting the entire classical heritage, but of a critical
selection of that which is necessary for progress.

To create something new, Ballet must first of all master the old.

Ballet accumulates the new slowly. At least two national theatres—the French and the Russian—labored for more than 50 years to make *Giselle* immortal.

The new grows within the old. And those who claim that they have created the new by severing all their ties with the old are seriously mistaken. There is only one alternative, either complete and unconditional negation of the old—and then defeat; or transformation on the basis of the old and creative development of its progressive trends—and then victory. This is proved by the whole course of the history of Ballet.

There can be no progress if there is no connection with the past. We are happy that the Soviet theatre follows the traditions elaborated by the great masters of Ballet in various countries and at various epochs. We are strong not only because we have retained and developed the best traditions of classical art, but also because we have used them critically in creating new ballets.

The best ballet classics have armed us with many principles of theory and practice.

Truly great creations boldly touch upon urgent problems, call for bigger things and therefore live as long as their theme moves the audience. Creations that do not touch man's mind or heart, that only please his eye, are doomed to early oblivion. These are not our words; they belong to the great Didelot. And here is the proof:

Dauberval's *La Fille mal Gardée* is still staged though it is over 150 years old. Despite its naïve and old-fashioned story, its theme is dear to the youth of all times and nations. His *Carefree Page* has long been forgotten, although it is just as talented a piece of work as any of his other ballets and although he based it on Beaumarchais' immortal comedy *The Marriage of Figaro*. This happened because Dauberval used only the "quid pro quo" of one "mad day" of his heroes. Its accusatory aspect, that is, the main idea of the comedy, was reduced to the minimum.

No matter how original the production may be, it will not be successful if there is nothing in it but beauty of form. The theatre exists for just one purpose—for showing a real man whose thoughts, feelings and action reflect life. That is why theatres that are not interested in man's spiritual qualities lose the right to call themselves theatres. These theatres, Stanislavsky told the young actors of the Bolshoi Theatre, "plunge into outer buffoonery, into outer affectations: they want a stage without a curtain, create unnatural decorations, seek for a false rhythm of action," forgetting the main thing —man's soul.

Literary classics time and again urged Russian Ballet to "seek for reality." Choreographers dreamed of that. Mikhail Fokine, for instance, said: "However distant and unrealistic the art of dancing may seem, it must reflect truth if it is to succeed." People like to quote Fokine, but often forget his credo.

The history of the ballet theatre is characterized by the search for a positive hero through whom it would be possible to express one's attitude to reality.

Take, for instance, the children of "the third estate" of the French revolutionary era—Lise and Colin from Dauberval's *La Fille mal Gardée*. They are confident that obstacles to man's happiness will collapse the moment they clash with man's desire and his ability to act. Or the heroes of the French romantic ballets of the 1830's and 1840's. They refuse to reconcile themselves to the world of cheap virtue and the cynic claim that money is all-powerful, and die in the unequal struggle with the milieu.

The squalor of life was the author's source of fantasy. That is why these authors of romantic ballets were attracted to fantastic themes. It was easier to write of one's dreams, to counterpose an imaginary hero to a "hero" out of life.

The fate of the heroine in *Giselle* was the fate of many in the France of the 1830's. Giselle is the blood-sister of Coralie in Balzac's *Lost Illusions* or of the heroes of Berlioz's *Symphonie Fantastique*. Different artists had different solutions for the problems agitating their minds. "Paris is a den of talents, a prison of minds, where faith in the fine things disappears and the fine things themselves perish." These words of Balzac are poetically reflected in *Giselle*.

The search for the new hero, started by the West-European theatre in the mid-19th century, was continued by Russian Ballet. The struggle for human dignity constituted the leit-motif of its best productions in the middle of the last century. Life is worth fighting and dying for—such is the conclusion reached by the heroes of

Chaikovsky's ballets. In his works there is no contrasting the hero to the crowd, as there is in the romantic French ballets of the first half of the 19th century (for instance, in *Esmeralda*). The theme that emerges is the one formulated by Pushkin—man's fate is that of his people. Soviet Ballet regards this as the main theme. The hero of Soviet Ballet wins the right to create his own happiness.

The best ballets of our classical heritage teach us to keep abreast of the times, to feel life's progress. That is why we guess in them the cherished hopes and aspirations of many generations. Each new epoch has its own keynote. If this contemporaneity of the theme is not understood—whatever the theme, be it legendary, historical or contemporary—then it is impossible to make the ballet true to life, artistic or long-lived.

We strive to bring out new ideas in old ballets. The ballet theatre's productions speak of love of man, boundless faith in his moral powers, hatred of everything that hampers his progress.

Before the Revolution there were those who urged Ballet's "deliverance" from dramaturgy. Soviet Ballet, on the contrary, stresses the dominant role of dramaturgy. For it is only when they are blended that dramaturgy, music and the dance acquire the qualities never known before.

The entire repertoire of Soviet Ballet—whether classics or modern works—is based to a certain degree on the classical dance. It has often been claimed that the system of the classical dance is outdated, unnatural and false. It has been said that the classical dance is incapable of embodying anything but the birds, insects and shadows of the romantic ballet. People went to the lengths of saying that it "was born on the parquet of a royal hall' and should be confined to oblivion along with "the old regime." Numberless experiments were carried out to find a substitute for the classical dance in sports, acrobatics, biomechanics, calisthenics, rhythmic plastics, etc. And yet no one has been able to find anything to replace the classical dance.

It has been proved that it is just as easy for a classical ballerina to dance barefoot and *sur les pointers,* in *tutu* or *tunique,* in ordinary dress or seminude, to do eccentric, folk, acrobatic or tap dancing. All the paths are open to a classical ballerina; for the opponent of the classical dance there is only one definite genre.

Classical dancing by no means belongs to just one country or just one epoch. It is the quintessence of the generalization of movements that man has been creating throughout the ages. It is immortal if it is regarded as a foundation for original images created by choreographers, musicians, ballerinas and dancers. Without the classical dance as the artistic language of Ballet there is no Ballet. There are no limits to the flexibility or volume of the classical dance, provided choreographers know how to use it, how to modernize and enrich it according to its laws and not their own whims.

There is no denying that when the classical dance is regarded as a collection of beautiful movements it loses its meaning. The use of ready-made school patterns for any situation and any image inevitably leads to formalism and naturalism. The most cunning pattern-creating is useless in the art of dancing, and is doomed to a short life, if there is no content.

In Soviet Ballet the classical dance has changed considerably. On the one hand, this is due to the novelty of the development of images and, on the other, to the development of folk dances.

Co-operation between Ballet and the folk dance had always been fruitful though complicated: the partitions separating them were too numerous. Only the most progressive dance artists saw in folklore an inexhaustible source of artistic wisdom and artistic renovation. In the Soviet theatre there is direct contact between Ballet and folk dance. Folk-dance ensembles are excellent links between folklore and Ballet. The former provides the latter with rich material with which to create new dance motifs. It supplies national color, enlivens characters, opens up new horizons for the development of the art of dancing, and makes it verisimilar.

But, however good old traditions may be, however powerful, they by themselves are not enough to constitute modern art. A new link must be added to the existing chain, a new step to the stairs that represent the history of Ballet. And that is why we rejoice that new productions constitute more than half of the Bolshoi Theatre ballet repertoire.

A successor to Russian Ballet, Soviet Ballet is different in quality, for it is a new art.

In the old days Ballet was just showy entertainment.

Now it strives to educate people—as Chaikovsky said it should. In the past the art of presentation dominated the art of emotion. Today every ballet requires a psychological analysis of the characters and situations.

In the past there were no social themes in Ballet. Today they are the leading themes. Before, it was only in the best ballets that there was complete co-operation between the musician, author and ballet masters. Today this co-operation is a law. The imperial theatres staged either West-European or Russian ballets. Today more and more works that are the national pride of the Soviet peoples are finding their way into the Bolshoi Theatre repertoire. Soviet Ballet on the Bolshoi stage is now multi-national.

The best ballets of the past were distinguished by their new ideas. The theatre of the 19th century, however, did not leave us a single ballet which directly reproduced contemporaneity. (*La Fille mal Gardée* which has come down to our days, is a creation of the 18th century.) Many theoreticians claimed that Ballet, like the opera, could not deal with contemporary things, and that if it did it was doomed to early death. Soviet Ballet has broken all time-lag concepts and has created a number of ballets on contemporary life, starting with *Red Poppy*. Some of the new ballets have remained in our repertoire, others proved short-lived, but they left a heritage in the shape of dance fragments that live to this very day on the concert stage. But more have remained and this allows us categorically to deny the claims that Ballet could not reflect contemporaneity.

When we speak of these ballets we mean such productions as *The Baby Stork, Svetlana, Youth, Gayaneh, Gulshen, Happy Shores* and *Tatyana*. The first-named has lived on our stage for 20 years and is one of the most popular of children's ballets.

Gayaneh is 15 years old and although the book leaves much to be desired, Khachaturyan's music and certain fragments appeal to the spectators as a true and poetical expression of contemporaneity.

Youth (music by Mikhail Chulaki, ballet master Boris Fenster) has been on the Maly Opera Theatre (Leningrad) repertoire for seven years and on and off in many other theatres of the country. It tells of several lads who grow to manhood during the Revolution, they start with playing soldiers and end up as soldiers of the Revolution. The choreographer succeeded in finding a new dance form that truthfully conveys the feelings of the heroes.

Happy Shores (music by Antonio Spadavekkia, ballet master Vladimir Burmeister) had its *première* at the Stanislavsky and Nemirovich-Danchenko Musical Theatre in 1948. It tells the story of young people bound together by friendship, love and camaraderie in the Great Patriotic War. There are many splendid moments in this ballet.

In 1947 Burmeister staged the ballet *Tatyana* at the Kirov Theatre in Leningrad. This ballet about young people (music by Alexander Krein) was not long-lived. But the scenes showing the front lines and the enemy rear were quite successful. It is a pity that no one has created a ballet in which the achievements of *Tatyana* could be further developed.

Gulshen (music by U. Gadzhibekov, ballet master Gamer Almas-zade), created by the Azerbaijan theatre, is a story about girls who grow cotton, about relations between young people who work selflessly to transform the desert into a garden.

There are many more gems that a balletomane could find in our other modern ballets, 16 of which have been created in the past ten years.

And still in general artistry and stage longevity they are inferior to many other Soviet ballets. There are many reasons for that. First of all, it is lack of experience in staging contemporary ballets. There are many successful miniatures and dances on modern themes, but very few full-length ballets. The new ballets evoke much discussion. The practice and theory of choreography will reveal the truth.

The ballet of the Bolshoi Theatre is striving to be worthy of its epoch and its people. The theatre is firmly resolved to make it a serious humanistic art and we believe that it is on the threshold of a promising future.

TRIUMPHAL AMERICAN DEBUT OF THE BOLSHOI BALLET

. . . so far 3,000,000 requests for tickets have been received by mail. . . .

N. Y. Times, April 14

In the jewel bright history of ballet, the name Bolshoi has a special splendor . . . The Bolshoi Ballet today is a magnificent and virtuoso studded dance troupe.

Life, February 23

. . . *Romeo and Juliet* "a great scenic dramatic pageant, overflowing with vitality, with choreographic invention, with miming, with spectacle, and emotion . . . Her (Ulanova's) Juliet is incredibly young. . . . What emerges is truer than reality itself . . . It is both an astonishing artistic achievement and a tremendously moving one . . . Lavrovsky is a master . . . The company is all stars; there is no doubt about that . . . The term "ballet" is likely to take on new meaning in these parts.

John Martin, N. Y. Times, April 17

An event of historic significance.

Walter Terry, N. Y. Herald-Tribune, April 17

. . . the most fought over tickets of theatrical history . . . Here were sumptuous scenes from Renaissance Italy that were like great paintings come to life.
The things that went on at the Metropolitan Opera House last night . . . cannot possibly be believed without being seen, and not very easily even then. . . . This fantastic company did everything technical except take off into outer space . . . exquisite poetry . . . practically every

girl in the company did the thirty-two fouettee's like crazy. . . . The men can turn like derviches and perform the most intricate classical steps while doing so. The girls, also, can get up in the air with or without provocation.

. . . Maya Plisetskaia, who is a vivid and beautiful hoyden does completely incredible things . . .

Raissa Struchkova . . . in . . . two breathtaking pas de deux, which exist almost entirely somewhere in the ether . . .

Still more was to come when this awe stricken reviewer reluctantly staggered down the aisle . . . Wow!

John Martin, N. Y. Times, April 17

. . . dancing that fell on the audience like a caress . . . a dazzling exhibition that tore the house apart.

Douglas Watt, Daily News, April 17

. . . Plisetskaya can best be described in the good old American slogan expression, "Wow!"

Walter Terry, N. Y. Herald-Tribune, April 17

. . . Mme. Ulanova worked her magic once again . . . [she made] . . . exploitation of technique seem like something only beginners would indulge in, capturing and communicating . . . sequential moods . . . Mme' Ulanova was, indeed, a wonder of dance.

Walter Terry, N. Y. Herald Tribune, May 1

One of the wonderful things in my theater going life happened at . . . the first performance of Swan Lake.

I cannot imagine how more skill, more zest and more beauty could be put upon a ballet stage.

. . . Last evening does not have to go in my memory book. It will glow in my memory as long as I have one.

John Patman, N. Y. Daily News, April 22, 1959

CPSIA information can be obtained at www.ICGtesting.com
Printed in the USA
BVOW11s1430250614

357369BV00012B/167/P